Playing on Words
a Guide to Luciano Berio's *Sinfonia*

ROYAL MUSICAL ASSOCIATION MONOGRAPHS, no. 1

General editor: David Fallows

This series is supported by funds made available to the Royal Musical Association from the estate of Thurston Dart, former King Edward Professor of Music in the University of London. The editorial board is the Proceedings Committee of the Association.

ROYAL MUSICAL ASSOCIATION
MONOGRAPHS

Playing on Words

a Guide to Luciano Berio's *Sinfonia*

DAVID OSMOND-SMITH

Lecturer in Music, University of Sussex

Royal Musical Association
London
1985

Published by the Royal Musical Association,
Registered office c/o Waterhouse & Co., 4 St Paul's
Churchyard, London EC4M 8BA

First published in 1985

British Library Cataloguing in Publication Data

Osmond-Smith, David
    Playing on words: a guide to Luciano
    Berio's Sinfonia. —— (Royal Musical
    Association monographs; no. 1)
    1. Berio, Luciano. Sinfonia
    I. Title   II. Series
    785.1'1'0924   ML410.B49/

ISBN 0 947854 00 2

This book is typeset by Goodfellow & Egan., Cambridge
The music examples were produced by Paul Courtenay

Printed in Great Britain by Henry Ling Ltd., The Dorset Press, Dorchester.
Design and Production in association with
Book Production Consultants, Cambridge.

Copies may be obtained from:

RMA Secretary (members only)
5 Church Street
Harston
Cambridge
CB2 5NP

Brian Jordan Music Books
12 Green Street
Cambridge
CB2 3JU

Contents

Preface

This study is indebted to several people. First, and most obviously, to Luciano Berio – not only because he provided the subject matter, but because he suggested to me many years ago that *Sinfonia* would repay close attention. He read a version of the resultant monograph several drafts back, and I must thank him for some all-too pertinent criticisms. I must also thank Joan Peyser for permission to reprint materials from an essay on Berio and Lévi-Strauss that appeared in *The Musical Quarterly*, and David Fallows for the benign editorial harassment without which this study would have made more arduous reading than it now does. None of these beneficent critics (cf. p.11 and 88) is responsible for the lacunae which I wish other analysts the joy of discovering.

I base my observations throughout on the printed score of *Sinfonia* issued in 1972 (Universal Edition, no.13783). This replaced a photocopy of the manuscript that was made available in 1969 (no.13f783). It corrected a number of errors in the manuscript version (though alas, not all) and also allowed Berio to rethink various matters of detail. In two instances where this reworking has rather wider formal implications the differences between the two versions have been noted; otherwise, I have confined myself to the 1972 score, regarded by the composer as definitive.

The aim of the study is not to give a complete description, but rather to pursue through the work all musically pertinent processes – to avoid, in other words, the tautology of reasserting in words what will be self-evident to the score-reader, while seeking to deploy analytical propositions where they are most useful to the musician: in suggesting a wider formal context within which individual details make sense.

1
Sinfonia and its Precursors

It is no accident that often I instinctively find myself working on different projects at the same time, amusing myself with one and sweating blood over another. But it is the tendency towards reunion that justifies the tendency to many-sidedness.

Luciano Berio[1]

Because Berio has found the simultaneous pursuit of two or three musical projects so congenial, his large-scale compositions have tended to take on a special role in relation to the rest of his work. They have provided the framework within which the exhilaration of these centrifugal enthusiasms could be countered by an act of synthesis. Such 'encyclopaedic' works recur throughout Berio's career: *Allez-Hop* (1959), *Epifanie* (1961), *Sinfonia* (1968), *Opera* (1970) and *Coro* (1975–6) are all to a greater or lesser extent examples of this tendency. But whereas *Allez-Hop* and *Epifanie* unite their disparate materials simply by placing them side by side, *Sinfonia* and *Coro* go beyond this, compelling different musical concerns to interact in the moment of composition itself. This is one of the primary reasons why they occupy so central a position within Berio's œuvre.[2]

In *Sinfonia* Berio synthesised several of his most long-standing concerns, making them literally 'sound together' as the title indicates. Throughout the sixties he had experimented with the resources of the human voice – not merely the range of articulation and tone that it could offer, but also the ways in which it could enhance the musical impact of language by emphasising, or indeed isolating its phonetic components. At first he had concentrated on the solo voice – in *Circles* (1960), *Epifanie* (1961) and above all *Sequenza III* (1965–6) – while exploring in a fairly straightforward way the juxtaposition of singing and speaking groups in *Passaggio* (1962)

---

[1] Berio 1985, p.100.

[2] It is also, no doubt, one of the reasons why *Sinfonia* in particular has attracted a good deal of commentary. The studies by Altmann and Hicks are referred to in the text, but the reader should also note Budde 1972, Dressen 1982, Flynn 1975, Jahnke 1973, Krieger and Stroh 1971, Ravizza 1974 and Stoianova 1974.

and *Laborintus II* (1965). But in *Sinfonia* he drew together these experiences in order to integrate them with an older, and in some ways more complex project: the search for satisfactory ways of extending the resources and traditions of the symphony orchestra. By using eight vocalists, the Swingle Singers, whose experience of jazz singing had accustomed them to close microphone work, he was able to blend their amplified voices into the orchestral textures – a deliberate reversal of the traditional polarity between 'choir' and 'orchestra'.

Sinfonia marked Berio's return to orchestral writing after a six-year gap (broken by *Chemins I* for harp and orchestra of 1965, which made only sparing use of its full orchestral resources). From the mid-fifties, when Berio first began to attract international attention, through to the last of the three orchestral *Quaderni*, all gathered together in *Epifanie*, his remarkable grasp of instrumental texture and colour had been widely acknowledged. This represented something of a personal triumph, for the wartime environment of his youth had been almost devoid of orchestral music.[3] It was only after he had begun his studies at the Milan Conservatorio in 1946, and particularly his composition studies with G. F. Ghedini (a composer also noted for his fine grasp of instrumentation), that he began a rapid and voracious assimilation of the European orchestral tradition. By 1954, when he produced *Nones*, his first major work for large orchestra, he was already in full command of the fragmented timbre-counterpoint typical of his more radical contemporaries.

But a more individual approach to the orchestra was quickly to follow, and it was one conditioned by Berio's work with electronic media in the Studio di Fonologia that he and Bruno Maderna had set up in Milan (1955). For here he was able to explore the superposition of layers of sonic material, each with its own complex internal structure. This affinity for a counterpoint of textures quickly transferred itself to his orchestral writing, where it was complemented by an expanded harmonic vocabulary that sought to go beyond the abstemious post-Webernian chiaroscuro of second- and seventh-based chords to a richer mix. *Allelujah* (1955–6) was his first attempt to come to grips with these possibilities, organising an orchestra minus upper strings into five groups – two of brass and percussion, one of pitched percussion and harps, and two of mixed woodwind and low strings – and using these to superpose layers of material. Dissatisfied with the results of this experiment, he reworked the piece as *Allelujah II* (1956–8), adding upper strings and a wider range of percussion to his resources, and working with more complex groupings of instruments, each separated from the other round the concert hall. Although this work allows for dialogue between relatively complex timbre-combinations (e.g. b.396–429, or the final pages), it is the superposition of distinct 'choirs', each with its characteristic timbre and texture, that most faithfully reflects Berio's

[3] cf. Berio 1985, p.45.

electronic experiences (e.g. b.39–60 and b.208–267, amongst others) and provides a foretaste of the approach that he was to bring to a more conventionally disposed orchestra in subsequent work. It was with the *Quaderni* – three sets of orchestral pieces subsequently interspersed with a cycle of vocal settings to form *Epifanie* – that this approach came to fruition. There Berio grouped his resources in a way that he was to take up with only minor modifications in *Sinfonia* six years later. The intervening *Chemins I* uses slighter resources but analogous principles.

In *Epifanie* there are four of each woodwind and brass family, save for six horns and a single tenor tuba. In *Sinfonia* grouping by four is all-pervasive (a reflection of the eight voices and of the consequent tendency towards four- and eight-part harmony), except that an alto and a tenor saxophone complement three upper double reeds and three bassoons respectively. *Chemins I*, grouping its instruments by threes, extends this 'choral' principle to keyboards with piano, celesta and harpsichord, used to articulate a rapid heterophony that is the direct ancestor of that played in the first movement of *Sinfonia* by an analogous group of piano, harp, electric harpsichord and electronic organ. *Epifanie* deploys three percussion groups separated as widely as possible from each other, but with several instruments in common (tam-tams, caisses claires, almglocken) to allow for dialogue. *Sinfonia* does the same, with tam-tams, snare drums and bongos in all three groups, but absorbs glockenspiel, marimbaphone and vibraphone into the groups rather than allocating them to separate players, as in *Epifanie*. In all three works there are eight instruments in each string section (save for *Epifanie*'s double basses); but as well as the two normal violin sections a third is seated in a row at the back of the orchestra, where they can provide a sustained background over which to project other layers.

Clearly, the presence of such carefully balanced strata of homogeneous timbre implies a marked interdependency between harmonic process, timbre and texture. A specific harmonic process may be marked out by a highly integrated selection of timbre and texture, as in *Epifanie A* where flutter-tongue flutes and muted trumpets (a favourite combination) explore a series of fixed pitch-fields at the opening and meander upward through the chromatic gamut at the end; or the start of *Epifanie B* where three separate layers – an ostinato-saturated major third from harps, pitched percussion and muted strings, whose complex inner life sets it off against quiet clarinet and trombone chords and violent lower string pizzicati – pursue partly independent existences. Conversely, a single harmonic 'object' may be passed from choir to choir, as in the opening section of *Epifanie C* and in the first and fourth movements of *Sinfonia*. The more complex harmonic aggregates that often occur in Berio's orchestral music likewise depend intimately on the presence of instrumental choirs. By the use of different dynamic contours for different groups the internal structure of such aggregates can be revealed, as in *Epifanie E* and the third movement of *Sinfonia*; and the extraordinary internal variety that can be achieved within that characteristic gesture, a dense chord used as a sharp, staccato attack, by subtle variations in interval distribution and more or less integrated timbre layers is apparent throughout *Epifanie* – notably in the latter half of **C**, and the proliferating stutter attacks of **D** – and in the third and fifth movements of *Sinfonia*. The technique is seen at its most concentrated in *Still* (1973), an orchestral study devoted entirely to soft, staccato aggregates.

Adding an extra 'choir' of singing and speaking voices seems no more than a logical extension of this approach. In practice, the integration of amplified voices and orchestra has sometimes proved difficult to achieve in the concert hall, but even so it was the most cogent solution that Berio had yet found to a familiar problem. He had presumably attempted to combine chorus and orchestra in *Nones*, first conceived as an oratorio setting W. H. Auden's poem of that name but then converted into a purely orchestral piece (1954). When he returned to the problem, working with Edoardo Sanguineti on the theatre piece *Passaggio* (1962), he chose to place a singing chorus in the pit with the orchestra and to distribute a speaking chorus around the auditorium. But his complex harmony did not benefit from the sort of projection that a conventional chorus must employ in such circumstances (the problem is a notoriously general one in twentieth-century vocal works). So when he and Sanguineti revived their collaboration in a work for smaller forces, *Laborintus II* (1965), he again separated speakers and singers, but specified that the latter should be used to microphone-singing, and have vibrato-less, non-operatic voices. It was this solution that he adapted to a larger scale when using the Swingle Singers in *Sinfonia*. Without their experience of amplified ensemble work, the synthesis that he achieved between orchestral sound and the vocal resources characteristic of his solo vocal works would have been a less inviting proposition.

Work in progress

If any single external influence is to be looked for in *Sinfonia*, and indeed in much else of Berio's work during the sixties, it is that not of another musician, but of James Joyce. That this should be so in relation to Berio's handling of texts is relatively unsurprising: the matter will be discussed in chapter two. But a more general principle, in part reflecting Joyce's own praxis over the last twenty years of his life, governs the major instrumental works produced during this period: the *Sequenzas*, *Chemins* and *Sinfonia*. In producing the various pieces of 'work in progress' that finally emerged as *Finnegans Wake*, Joyce elaborated on a demotic Anglo-Irish basis an extraordinary tissue of multilingual puns, adding layer upon layer of associations. The texts often underwent several revisions, usually in the direction of greater complexity, sometimes obliterating the

original proposition in the process. Certain texts were thus published in several successive versions before the *Wake* finally
appeared. The process could, in theory, have gone on and on:
Finnegans Wake is by nature intransigently unfinishable.

Berio began to explore a parallel approach with his *Chemins I* for
harp and orchestra of 1965. He had produced his *Sequenza II* for harp
in the previous year and, wishing to elaborate its material further,
decided to add extra instrumental layers on top of it. The process
was entirely compatible with his general approach to the orchestra,
save that now one layer was complete before the others were added.
Several more *Sequenzas* were produced in rapid succession in the
mid-sixties, but it was not until *Sequenza VI* for viola (1967) that
Berio once again sensed the potential for elaboration, producing in
Chemins II for viola and chamber ensemble (1967) a work whose
density of texture frequently obliterates the contours of the original
solo line. The process was compounded in 1968, when *Chemins III*
added an extra orchestral layer to *Chemins II*; and it was taken to a
logical conclusion when the original solo line was entirely absorbed
in an orchestral reworking: *Chemins IIb*.[4] It is these works that
provide the context for *Sinfonia*, for here, too, pre-existent musical
texts are subjected to elaboration. But to understand how these processes help to shape the work it is necessary to review its large-scale
structure, which is as much conditioned by Berio's relish for creating
a unity out of the most improbable diversity as it is by a search for
organic proliferation.

An overview of *Sinfonia*

The deliberate combination of heterogeneous materials is common
to several of Berio's works of the later sixties. *Questo vuol dire che*
(1968), close in spirit to the 'happening' so prevalent at the time,
displays this preoccupation in its most freewheeling form: there is
no score, and Berio provides only a tape and certain other materials
to be coordinated as the individual performance is prepared. *Opera*
(1970) unites disparate dramatic schemes – a mental hospital, the
sinking of the Titanic, a resetting of part of Striggio's libretto for
Monteverdi's *L'Orfeo* – all linked by the underlying theme of death.
It also brings together, as the title punningly suggests, several
autonomous works and makes them function within a dramatic
framework. But so far as the synthesis of disparate elements is concerned, *Sinfonia* is the most rigorous and technically adventurous of
these works. For where *Opera* can look to its dramatic framework to
help hold the musical components together, *Sinfonia* achieves
synthesis by purely musical means.

It takes three disparate projects: (a) a setting of fragments from
Claude Lévi-Strauss's *Le cru et le cuit* in which verbal sense, at best
only partly perceptible, gives way to a gradual build-up of nervous,

---

[4] For a fuller discussion of both Joyce's and Berio's procedures, see Osmond-
Smith 1983.

5

rapid melody; (b) a reworking of the commemorative chamber piece *O King* (1967) in which, on the basis of a cyclic pitch sequence that generates its own harmonic environment, disjointed phonemes gradually connect to form the name of Martin Luther King; and (c) a commentary on the scherzo from Mahler's Second Symphony that superposes upon the original 'text' other materials of differing harmonic densities, some derived from the orchestral repertoire, others invented by Berio himself. On the surface these have little to do with each other (apart from certain semantic congruences to be discussed below), and the gong strokes that mark the passage from movement to movement seem to be their only common feature. Yet all three reflect a common concern: the recuperation of a vocabulary of third-based chords.

This was no new preoccupation for Berio, but it was one that was moving to an increasingly central position in his work, as is clear from such direct antecedents as *Sequenza IV* for piano (1966) and *Laborintus II*. In the first movement of *Sinfonia*, third-based chords provide no more than a static background to the detailed exploration of vocal and instrumental texture; but in the second movement a harmonic alternation between two whole-tone harmonic areas – each most characteristically defined by a major third plus a tone – lies at the core of a complex and constantly shifting harmonic network. Inevitably, the third movement brings a related set of harmonic possibilities into play when it superposes denser layers of commentary upon a diatonic original. At first, Berio had considered rounding off this sequence with a quiet epilogue – the present fourth movement – which would complement both the harmonic vocabulary of the second movement and the play with fixed harmonic 'objects' of the first. It was thus that it was first performed and recorded.[5] But these experiences convinced him of. the need for a genuine synthesis between those disparate projects – an idea to which he had already given thought, though he had not fully worked it out – and in the early months of 1969 he produced the fifth movement which reworks, concurrently, materials from all the previous movements, thereby adding a further layer of meaning to the title of the work.

A work for voices also implies a semantic content and structure. Although within each of the first three movements this is fairly sharply defined, the relations between the movements depend upon two generalized themes: water and death. The fragments that Berio

---

[5] The recording, CBS 61079/606259, with the Swingle Singers and the New York Philharmonic Orchestra conducted by the composer, was the only one readily available until a complete performance was issued in 1985 with Swingle II and the Orchestre National de France conducted by Pierre Boulez. The earlier performance is an essential document, particularly because the vivacity and raw edge of the Swingle Singers gave to the work an excitement that later and more professionally polished ensembles could not easily match. But at the same time it has propagated a lopsided and slightly inconsequential view of the work owing to the absence of the final movement.

takes from Lévi-Strauss's *Le cru et le cuit* to provide the text for the first and last movements derive from myths recounting the origins of water. From them, Berio extracts a single image, the 'héros tué', with which to close the first movement and to usher in his tribute to the assassinated Martin Luther King. Both themes coexist in the background to the third movement, for the scherzo of Mahler's Second Symphony started life as a song about St Anthony of Padua (another preacher, in this context a rather futile one) delivering a sermon to the fishes. Berio responds with a number of aqueous quotations: among them are Debussy's *La Mer*, 'Farben' from Schoenberg's Op.16, and a single moment at the very heart of the work where the two themes meet in the drowning scene from *Wozzeck*. But in its symphonic version, Mahler's movement became part of a programme of death and resurrection, even if the detailed significance of this movement as a moment of 'disgust for all being and becoming'[6] is not particularly germane to Berio's project, save as a reflection of the text. This is extracted from Samuel Beckett's *The Unnamable* and also evokes death of a sort, for its narrator is trapped in a Dantesque limbo, attempting to talk himself into oblivion. The fourth movement returns to the image of spilt blood with its 'rose de sang', and the final movement, though initially supplying some of the missing pieces in the jigsaw puzzle of myth fragments set up by the first movement, ultimately turns back to the overriding theme of 'la vie brève' and human mortality.

[6] cf. p.54.

2
Mythologiques

When Berio chose to use the 'overture' to the 'Sirens' chapter from Joyce's *Ulysses* as the starting-point for his *Thema: Omaggio a Joyce* (1958), he brought into creative focus two ways of operating upon a pre-existent text that were to be central to much of his vocal music over the next decade. The first of these operations was provided by Joyce himself, for he had built the opening section of the 'Sirens' chapter by extracting fragments from the ensuing narration (of Mr Bloom's late lunch in the Ormond bar to a background of singing around the pub piano) and building from them a stream of images, vivid in their isolation, that interact to create not only implicit meanings quite divorced from their original context but also a word-music of their own.

In *Thema* Berio took the process a stage further, allowing that word-music its autonomy by breaking down the text-fragments into their phonetic components, and using the articulatory relationships between them as the basis for a musical structure. In this instance he realized the piece electronically, using recordings of the text made by Cathy Berberian;[1] but he was soon using symbols from the phonetic alphabet[2] in his vocal scores as a means of continuing the investigation – briefly in *Circles*, but far more richly and thoroughly in *Sequenza III* for voice. He thus had at his disposal two disparate principles for organizing phonetic materials: sequences extracted from, and 'standing for' the original order of the text; and sequences derived from simple games played out within the matrix of articulatory positions provided by the phonetic alphabet. The tension between these two kept his vocal music balanced on the borderline between sound and sense. That tension was to find one of its most elegant resolutions in *O King* (1967), incorporated as the second movement of *Sinfonia*. A more technical discussion of how Berio handles phonetic materials may therefore be deferred to chapter three, where that movement is analysed.

But although phonetic materials, rather less rigorously handled,

---

[1] See Berio 1959.
[2] International Phonetic Association 1949.

also make an important contribution to the surface texture of *Sinfonia*'s opening movement, it is Joyce's own technique of verbal fragmentation that provides the essential background to the piece. Berio had already returned to the example of the 'Sirens' chapter when collaborating with Sanguineti on *Laborintus II*, written to celebrate the 700th anniversary of Dante's birth. Sanguineti's poetic style – in part inspired by the experiments of Pound and Eliot – frequently juxtaposed discontinuous fragments, sometimes in different languages, and thus lent itself readily to the incorporation of elements from Dante's texts. As in Joyce, these fragments, often chosen to represent salient features of the original text, developed a strikingly individual resonance in isolation and combined to generate new and sometimes unexpected meanings.[3]

This technique, only modestly developed in *Laborintus II*, became absolutely central to the first movement of *Sinfonia*, for here Berio was at work on a text that would not immediately suggest itself as a candidate for musical setting: Claude Lévi-Strauss's anthropological study of South American Indian mythology, *Le cru et le cuit*.[4] Like Joyce, Lévi-Strauss was passionately devoted to music, though he invoked it not merely as an ingredient of language's poetic impact but as an analytical tool. In *Le cru et le cuit*, the first volume in a series of four entitled *Mythologiques*, he used the structures of Western classical music as metaphors for the transformational relations that he was seeking to demonstrate between the myths of different tribal groups.[5] His book therefore offers a series of myth narrations transcribed into a vivid and lucid French, interspersed with analytical commentary that extracts salient images in order to show their transformational relations to other myths from different sources. Berio's work in looking for isolated images that will 'stand for' a complex whole is thus already half-done by Lévi-Strauss's mode of analysis.

The sources of Berio's text

The mythical universe that Lévi-Strauss sets out to explore gravitates towards no central point. Consequently, the myth that provides him with his starting-point is arbitrarily chosen (see *Le cru et le cuit*, p.10). It is a Bororo myth concerning the origin of rain (and featuring as

[3] Examples of the process are analysed in Osmond-Smith 1981, pp.234–7. Sanguineti's text for *Laborintus II* is reprinted in Sanguineti 1983.
[4] All references in the text are to the original French edition, Lévi-Strauss 1964. The reader of the English translation (1970) will locate almost all page references by subtracting 6 from the original reference – except in the introduction to the work, where 8 should be subtracted.
[5] As Lévi-Strauss explains in Nattiez 1973, p.5, this in turn was the fruit of a long-standing frustration at not being able to compose music. By book four of *Mythologiques* – *L'homme nu* – the procedure had clarified itself into the hypothesis that music and myth have played complementary roles in the history of humanity, and that as the functions of myth fade away in post-Renaissance Europe, so their role is taken over by music.

part of its complex story the theft of a triad of musical instruments, a penance that the hero has to undergo for having raped his mother), thereafter labelled M.1. Lévi-Strauss then takes a further Bororo myth concerning the creation of rivers and lakes, M.2, and demonstrates that it is a transformation of M.1. This opposition between 'eau céleste' and 'eau terrestre' is central to Lévi-Strauss's argument, for in the opening section of chapter four he is able to demonstrate that a Sherenté myth concerning the origin of earthly water, M.124, is a transformation of M.1, and a Kayapo myth concerning the origin of heavenly water, M.125, is a transformation of M.2. Thus M.124 and M.125 reverse the transformational relationship between M.1 and M.2 – a situation summarized by Lévi-Strauss (p.217) in the diagram reproduced as example 1, where the Sherenté and Kayapo myths are resumed under the more generic Gé grouping.

Ex. 1

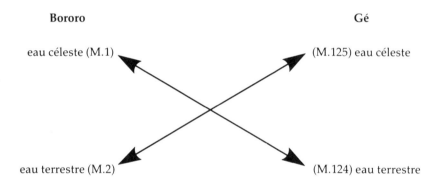

It is this structure that provides Berio with his framework. Setting aside M.1 for the moment, he starts his movement with the opening and closing paragraphs of M.124, which are heard up to **C**, and finishes the vocal section of the movement (**H3**–10)[6] with phrases from a diagram in which Lévi-Strauss analyses the transformational relationship between M.2 and M.125 ('arbre résorbée', etc: p.215). The fundamental opposition of example 1, 'eau céleste/terrestre', is also used as a background for much of the previous material, appearing at **F9** and running through to **H**. Above it, a single voice announces the opposition 'pluie douce de la saison sèche'/'pluie orageuse de la saison des pluies'. This comes from another of Lévi-Strauss's diagrams (p.221) in which he summates his conclusions about the distinction made by the Bororo between different sorts of rain, having first demonstrated that the Bororo myth of 'pluie douce', M.127, is a transformation of the Kayapo myth of 'pluie orageuse', M.125.

[6] All references to the score are by rehearsal letter plus bar number.

Berio has thus provided himself with two sets of materials concerned with water. In between them he puts a brief section deriving from an opposing element: fire. Immediately after his discussion of 'pluie douce' and 'pluie orageuse', Lévi-Strauss recalls a myth, M.9, which is linked to the myths of example 1 by the fact that each features three important objects or elements (the three musical instruments of M.1 being one such triad). In M.124 three types of alimentary detritus (which are therefore 'anti-nourritures') are used by three beneficent animals in turn, in order to hide the hero from a pursuing crocodile. Corresponding to these in M.9 is another series of three inedible objects – rock, hard wood and rotten wood – that cry out to the hero on his journey. Once again, Berio takes his materials from a diagram (p.161) analysing these and other triadic relations. The 'appel bruyant' of E2 onward is that of rock and hard wood to which the hero must respond; the 'doux appel' of the same section is that of rotten wood to which the hero mistakenly responds, thereby bringing death to mankind. In turn, M.9 is linked to M.127 and M.125, for Lévi-Strauss posits a correspondence between 'pluie douce', 'pluie orageuse' and 'rivières et lacs' (i.e. earthly waters such as those of M.2 and M.124) and three forms of food that are the opposites of the 'anti-foods' of M.9 (p.161).

Ex. 2

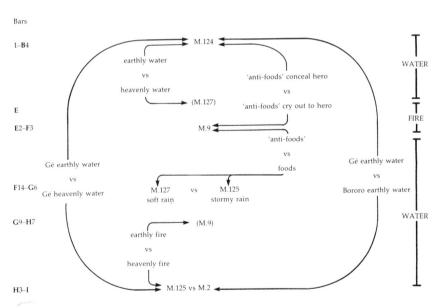

Berio has thus drawn from *Le cru et le cuit* a closed universe of interrelated myths, summarized in example 2. The simple Water–Fire–Water sequence that they create is slightly complicated by two brief insertions, here shown in parentheses: materials from M.127 ('pluie douce' at E) preface M.9; and the triad of 'anti-nourritures' – 'bois pourri', 'bois dur', 'roc' – from M.9 is introduced fleetingly in the midst of the second Water section at **H**. Both are there as vehicles for Joycean semantic games, to be discussed below on p.14. But the second insertion also finds Berio amusing himself by extending Lévi-Strauss's own game: M.9 concerns the beneficent 'feu terrestre', M.125 speaks of the destructive 'feu céleste' – the thunderbolt which kills many people. Although Lévi-Strauss acknowledges the opposition in theory (p.217), he does not expand upon it in relation to these two myths. A similar extension of Lévi-Strauss's approach can be found in Berio's treatment of M.124, the only extended myth narration in the movement. The narrator starts his story at b.6, impeded by a curious semantic stutter that hints at fragmentation to come, but is almost immediately interrupted by a taboo-imposing orchestra just as he is about to recount the group rape of a mother by her sons. Once the orchestral tumult has subsided, Berio jumps straight to the last paragraph of the myth – unexplored by Lévi-Strauss – which functions as a speakable version of the unspeakable first paragraph: the sons now plunge themselves into the sea and are, as a result, not vilified but purified. Lévi-Strauss's comment, 'ce mythe nous retiendra longtemps', follows – a remark not immediately true so far as *Sinfonia* is concerned, for we move straightaway to other material, but an apt enough prophecy of the last movement.[7]

Isolated words and their function

The inchoate background out of which these fragments of narration and commentary emerge is built from isolated words and phonetic materials. The latter are in large measure free from any obligation to the structure of Lévi-Strauss's argument (though they all derive from his text) and will be discussed below. Many of the isolated words are also simply echoes of the text. But two of these words, 'pluie' and 'eau', acquire a more independent existence, and they are joined by three others, 'sang', 'feu' and 'vie', that are not otherwise present in the fragments that Berio has chosen to use. With the exception of 'sang', all of these represent one of the basic themes of the myths discussed above, and they are deployed as background up to the point where the relevant myth assumes the foreground. This is most evident in the case of M.9, whose materials appear just after **E**. M.9 accounts not only for the origin of fire but also for the brevity of human life. 'Feu' is much in evidence from the opening and continues up to **E** where it disappears. Likewise 'vie' is strikingly introduced between **D** and **E** never to appear again. In accordance with the same principle 'sang', not an important theme but nevertheless a striking image in M.2 and M.125, appears frequently throughout the movement until **H**, where it disappears and the myths in question take over. 'Eau' and 'pluie' are more pervasive, as might be expected, being used consecutively to accompany the

---

[7] For a more detailed analysis of the relations between the text of this movement and Lévi-Strauss's book, see Osmond-Smith 1981.

opening narration, but disappearing during the Fire section. 'Eau' then reappears at F5, ushering in the water myths that follow.

Certain of these words are emphasized as rapidly alternating pairs. Further delving into Lévi-Strauss's text reveals almost all of these as distant echoes of what were originally narrative elements. Granted that it is only a passing image in M.2 and M.125, 'sang' seems to assume an unduly insistent role in the movement, albeit one that underlies the death theme running through the whole of *Sinfonia*. But it appears in opposition to 'feu' both during the opening narration and at D, and if one takes the two words as respectively standing for 'le cru' and 'le cuit' their function is quickly clarified: as a proper preface to the whole movement before A, and as an introduction to M.9 materials at E, in which myth the jaguar initiates a young Indian into the delights of cooked meat (previously unknown to mankind). Similarly, 'sang' reappears in alternation with 'eau' at F5, ushering in M.125 where the action is precipitated by the hero's failure to wash the blood of a hunted animal from his hands.

Phonetic materials

These isolated words also provide the phonetic materials that form a backdrop to the first Water section. It is mainly the vowels that are used – [o] from 'eau', [ø] from 'feu', [i] from 'pluie' and 'vie', [a] from 'sang'[8] – thus creating a suitably fluid background. But apart from the [v] of 'vie', all the sounding consonants are also represented. From E, the phonetic materials become less independent, echoing the verbal fragments of the Fire section, after which they disappear altogether. The Fire section also introduces random mutterings that mirror the rapid wind oscillations. No more than a detail here, they will reappear in the fourth movement as an important cadential feature. Throughout these first two sections two other vocal sounds are used: ? indicating an undifferentiated vowel sound, and + indicating singing with closed lips.

The poetics of fragmentation

It will be clear by now that there is a deliberate gap created by Berio between the (mytho)logic of his source and the semantic impact of the work either as score or as performance – a gap which not even the most expert listener can bridge. Jean-Jacques Nattiez records a conversation with Lévi-Strauss as follows: 'si la *Sinfonia* de Berio utilise des passages de *Le cru et le cuit*, notre auteur [i.e. Lévi-Strauss] a l'impression que son texte a été ramassé par hasard, qu'il n'est pour rien dans l'œuvre'.[9] This impression is hardly surprising, however inaccurate in point of fact. It is possible for Berio to take a musical, time-based structure such as the Mahler scherzo of the

---

[8] A phonetician would have added a nasal ~: perhaps the [a] instead derives from the narration, where it constantly recurs: 'avait', 'adultes', 'appelait', 'Asaré', etc.

[9] Nattiez 1973, p.6.

third movement and to fragment it in a manner at times equally ruthless, without the knowledgeable listener becoming entirely disoriented. But Lévi-Strauss has created a complex conceptual structure which, although it must perforce be expounded sequentially, is fundamentally synchronic (and necessitates constant cross-reference in the text to make itself understood). This castle in the air cannot survive fragmentation; nor indeed does Berio intend it to. Instead, he follows Joyce's example, isolating individual images in order to give full resonance to their poetic impact. Lévi-Strauss may properly say of his book that 'ce livre sur les mythes est-il, à sa façon, un mythe' (p.14), but it is a quite different sort of myth, one that is the fruit of an attempt to 'reduire des données apparement arbitraires à un ordre' (p.18). By fragmenting that order into a further set of 'données apparement arbitraires', Berio proposes to release the poetic potential of Lévi-Strauss's language, to restore ambiguity where coherence had supervened. (And the present attempt at exegesis offers a further swing of the pendulum.)

Isolated phrases can give rise, here, as in Joyce's 'Sirens' chapter, to new semantic affinities. It is this possibility which prompts Berio to insert a water myth fragment at the start of the Fire section, and a fire myth fragment in the second Water section – in both instances creating a fleeting combination that is the very opposite of their relationship in Lévi-Strauss's text. Thus when, at E, the 'pluie douce' of M.127 is juxtaposed with the 'doux appel' of M.9, the listener might well suppose the latter to be a poetic attribute of the former. In fact, as we have already seen, the two are in direct opposition: the 'doux appel' emanates from the 'bois pourri' which is the 'anti-nourritures' opposite of the 'plants cultivés' with which the 'pluie douce' is associated; and when the 'bois pourri' is finally named at H, it is associated with the 'arbre résorbé sous l'eau' of M.2. Again, the listener might well suppose that the latter consisted of the former. In fact, the 'arbre résorbé sous l'eau', far from rotting, is instead the bringer of life-giving water to the vegetable realm, whilst the 'bois pourri' is the bringer of early death to human beings.

Berio also poeticizes the text by emphasising its musical values: simple phonetic oppositions, assonance and rhyme. Most of these are perfectly obvious, and need no analytical commentary; but it is worth underlining the overall sequence. The narrations of the first Water section are complicated by repeating certain words or phrases several times, creating a semantic stutter that galvanizes the whole of the vocal section into nervous life. These repetitions underline front–back oppositions between the final vowels of successive fragments thus treated: 'il y avait' (front) versus 'plusieurs' (back), 'aujourd'hui' (front) versus 'vers le fin' (mid-mouth), etc. After vowel oppositions, the Fire section from E to F focuses on vowel identity through the recurrent [i] of 'vie' and 'pluie'. Vowel identity gives way to consonant identity in the second Water section (F8–H7)

with its recurrent 's's and 'r's, and both identities are finally sub-
sumed in the recurrent syllable 'tu' at the close of this section
('tuant', 'tué', 'rituelle': cf. H8–11).

Coherence as structure

Berio compounds the listener's estrangement from the structural
relations of Lévi-Strauss's text by presenting different fragments
simultaneously, forcing him to grasp at momentarily comprehensible gestures within the general *mêlée*. This fascination with
working at the very limits of coherence is confined to a verbal level
in the first movement, but it is to proliferate into other, strictly
musical levels in the third and fifth movements. Even so, different
levels of comprehensibility are available to Berio as an element of
musical form, and he makes full use of them. The crucial factors
here are the semantic 'completeness' of each piece of material, the
number of superposed verbal events, and the various modes of
articulation from singing to whispering. Bringing these together,
three clear-cut sections emerge between the start and I, where the
voices break off. In the first, stretching to E, two passages of continuous myth narration for solo voice are flanked by passages con-
sisting of phonemes and isolated words. Although stylised by the
use of fixed intonation and internal repetition, and although
interrupted by occasional outbursts from other voices and eventually
plagued by a manic echo, these narrations constitute the most lucid
moment in the movement, and stand out clearly against multifarious
background murmurings. The odd isolated word emerges from the
phonetic background in the surrounding episodes; but here attention is focused on vowel timbre and rhythmic texture. From E
through to the fourth bar of F a new semantic texture is developed
in which, with continuous narration having disappeared and with
phonetic materials taking a subsidiary role, a polyphony between
sung fragments is established. But with long, melismatic vowels and
two or three different lines superposed, the ear must strain to catch
at any meaning. The final section however returns to the comparative clarity of a single speaking voice versus the other seven in a
part-whispered, part-spoken unison, although by now the material
consists entirely of fragments and isolated words. Clearly, these
three types of semantic texture correspond directly with the alternating themes of Water–Fire–Water concealed beneath their surface.

Musical structure

The deliberately parsimonious musical materials deployed during
the vocal part of the movement simply underline this tripartite
division. They also establish a harmonic language that is to per-
meate much of the score, a language based upon accumulations of
thirds. The first Water section is underpinned by an alternation,
three times repeated, between two such chords. The first of these is
an eight-part chord that establishes a model for much of the har-

monic writing to follow with its wider spacing at the bottom (here, typically, a fifth) underpinning a chain of thirds (diminished seventh and fifth chords superposed); the second is a four-part chord. They are set out in white note-heads in example 3. The return of chord 1 at **A** and **C** introduces another of Berio's harmonic preoccupations. For the surrounding orchestral parts now flesh it out to chromatic saturation, expanding the third-chain and shifting the bare fifth at the root of the chord down a fifth to produce the additions notated in black note-heads in example 3.[10] Since two notes, c and eb, are common to chords 1 and 2, it follows that two others are missing. These two notes – f and $g\sharp$ – are used to initiate additions to chord 2 at its first recurrence: the $g\sharp$ at the bass of a downward extension of the chord at **A9**, the f initiating a chord of all the other missing pitches save bb four bars later (cf. ex. 3). When chord 2 returns for the third time, an added bass line begins with $f\,ab$ (**C5**), while the high flute d prepares for brief saturation at **C11**. This simple principle of a basic harmonic layer being surrounded by other layers derived from its chromatic complement will recur, in more sophisticated form, throughout the rest of the work.

Ex. 3

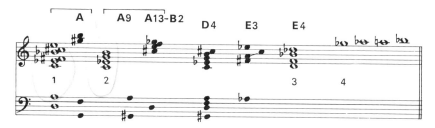

Such harmonic simplicity allows for a rich play of textures. They are of no great complexity, for the constant superpositions all derive from quavers and triplet quavers; but again they provide simple examples of devices that will constantly recur. Berio's delight in seeking out correspondences between vocal and instrumental sound is immediately apparent when the full orchestra enters at **A**. Rapid crescendos and decrescendos within the chord establish an analogy between, on the one hand, voices playing with vowels and, on the other hand, an octet of trumpets, horn and trombones each playing with a different mute. The subsequent resolution onto chord 2 from **A4**, and its parallel passage from **C4**, both allow Berio to demonstrate how his wind and brass sections resolve into four-part choirs. The introduction of the upper range of complementary pitches at **A13** provides a first example of another constantly used device

[10] Readers of the earlier facsimile score (1969) should note that Berio originally wrote this chord with a $g\sharp$ in the bass and a $g\natural$ at the top of the treble stave, thus emphasising the logic of superposed diminished chords. He then revised the score before definitive publication in 1972 so as to conserve the characteristic fifth at the base of the chord, and to contrast with the $g\sharp$–based addition to chord 2 (cf. **A9**).

when a sforzando line – here just two notes in the trumpet – leaves behind its own harmonic echo (in flutes 1 and 2); and at **B** the sopranos profit from this new harmonic field to initiate a further characteristic gesture, a nervous staccato line permutating a few fixed pitches.

At **D4** Berio closes the first Water section with a hybrid chord, a cross between the extended forms of chords 1 and 2.[11] A transitional passage (E1–3) of shifting harmonies, setting the juxtaposition of fire and water materials discussed above (p.11), stabilizes momentarily on a diminished seventh chord over an alien ab, emphasising once more chains of minor thirds. It then gives way to a new, stable chord of two superposed minor thirds, chord 3 in example 3, upon which the remainder of the Fire section is based. Its characteristic texture is no longer one of repeated attacks, as in the first section, but rather of oscillation – uneven in the voice parts, consistently rapid in clarinet and saxophone. Against these, piano and harpsichord execute ornamental flurries, loosely focused upon the notes of the chord. Both of these features are to assume a more significant role once the voice parts have exhausted their materials.

At **E8** the first soprano leaps to a high g, directly anticipating her analogous gesture at the climax of the second movement (cf. **II, E9**). Here, however, she opens up the register that will provide the harmonic basis for the second Water section, while at the same time placing it 'beyond the reach' of the other voices, who from now on will speak. That harmonic basis is quickly established: a $gb–bb$ cluster, chord 4, saturated save for the g which introduced it. It completes a simple harmonic process, easily seen by comparing chords 1 to 4 in example 3. Chords 1 and 3 are governed by minor thirds, chords 2 and 4 by major thirds. Chords 2, 3 and 4 each conserve one third relationship from chord 1 – with chord 4 transposing the lower major third in chord 1 up an octave, and the borrowed third from chord 1 providing the only minor third in chord 2.

The inner articulations of chord 4 recall those of the first Water section, as do the changes of timbre as it is passed from one high wind choir to the next. But this is no longer the only focus of interest. For what were no more than ornamental flurries in the Fire section have now consolidated themselves into a nervous, widely leaping melodic line articulated by the strings, with heterophonic commentary from woodwinds and occasional brass. Initially this is based upon a rotating pitch sequence, which becomes increasingly fragmented and dispersed as a manic orchestral unison establishes itself. The eighteen-note sequence is set out in example 4 in its most typical order (based entirely upon the string line up to I3, though the wind elaborations are in the main quite easily derived from it). As might be expected, the pitches employed are the chromatic

[11] Its dual nature would have been even clearer in the earlier version: see note 10 above.

Ex. 4

complement of chord 4 – save for $c\sharp$, which is to find a different
function. They are deployed so as to form a pattern of internal
permutation and substitution within its two halves (indicated by ⌣)
and a retrograde structure pivoting around the final e of the first half
(indicated by ⌐). The retrograde demands a g as the penultimate
pitch class of the first half; but if it were also to be retained as a
component of the last group of four, too radical a dominance would
be achieved by d and g, each occurring four times where the others
occur twice. Accordingly, Berio replaces it with an $e\flat$, thus establishing a recurrent d–$e\flat$ coupling which is to act as an idée fixe throughout this section, even when the original pitch set is lost. The various
realizations of the sequence are set out below, running through to
the point where at best only permuted two- or three-note fragments are discernible within the continuous hemidemisemiquaver
movement. The first four rotations of this sequence – two complete,
two fragmentary – plus their heterophonic commentaries amalga-

mate with the spoken texts and the polyrhythmic cluster articulations to form a complex, layered texture that is completed by an independent bass line in which the c♯/d♭ absent from both cluster and melodic line is prominent. At first (**F4**) a nervous staccato bass permutating d♭, d and e♭ (and later adding g and c) underlines the setting of the 'eau céleste/terrestre' opposition and the M.127 materials – developing further the idiom introduced by the sopranos at **B**. But as the text moves on to the interpolated fire myth materials ('bois pourri/dur', etc.) the woodwind heterophony plunges downward to establish a low c♯ that initiates an independent line. A further layer is established a bar later, at **H**, where the final e♭ of statement two of the pitch cycle generates an independent, gradually quickening oscillation between e♭ and d♭ in horns and trombones. What is here but a single element, helping to prepare the forthcoming climaxes at I4 and I9, will reappear in the fourth movement as the central harmonic focus.

All of these layers except one are to be swept quickly away. Voices dissolve into noise at I2 and disappear. Two bars before, string glissandi have expanded chord 4 to a saturated fifth, e–b, which erupts into a first climax at I4. It is answered immediately by a c from the horns; keyboards reply with the opening d and e♭ of the pitch cycle, plus a high d♭; and, thus prompted, the cluster expands into a vast agglomeration at I9 that completely saturates the chromatic gamut from the piccolo's a♭ in altissimo down to the cellos' d♭, and then proceeds by steps of two through to six semitones to the bass tuba's f. Such monster aggregates are not to be heard again until the central section of the third movement, where they become a major feature. Here, however, the chord rapidly dissolves, leaving only harp, piano and harpsichord who have taken over from strings as the main bearers of the melodic line.

This trio at first articulates a melodic line still bound by the pitch cycle (cf. ex. 4, cycle 5). But by J5 it has begun to permutate pitch order; and although a recognizable relationship is regained from J8–10, it is cut short by a c–f♯ interruption and, retaking the start of the cycle, freewheels off into an autonomous melodic line. Although this continues to gravitate around the pitch cycle's d and e♭, it employs all pitch classes except a. Its oscillating patterns create a phantasmagoric virtual counterpoint of tone and semitone steps not unlike that which Berio had explored extensively in *Sequenza VI* for viola of the previous year, a similarity underlined from **K** on when upper strings realise the implicit harmonies as tremolando chords. The melodic line gathers both momentum and weight, being scored first as a unison, then in octaves. After a horn interruption at J20 the thickening process continues through parallel fifths (**K4**), triads (**K7**) and dominant sevenths (**L**) into discordant contrary motion (**L4**) and thereafter saturation.

The purpose of excluding a from the melodic line becomes clear as this accumulative process reaches its first climax at **L**. The tutti is answered by a solo piano with a spread chord whose top note is a, and whose other notes, d b $g\sharp$ f, form the diminished seventh chord not represented in chord 1. Three times the piano answers the full orchestra with this chord before resolving into chord 1. The piano broods further on this relationship in L5–6; and then, as the voices re-enter with chord 1 over a saturated orchestral diminuendo, it launches forth in an independent rhapsodic vein that is to appear once more at the start of the last movement. The orchestral explosions at last exhaust themselves, leaving a solitary flute at L11 which, as the voices resolve chord 1 into chord 2, completes the chromatic field with f and $a\flat$, plus a low $f\sharp$ echoing that of the piano. Over chord 2 a final orchestral flurry leaves chord 1 in the strings. This then evaporates, and the three gongs close the movement as they had opened it.

3
'O King'

Berio produced the chamber version of *O King* in 1967 in response to a commission from the Aeolian Players and as a tribute to the memory of Martin Luther King, whose name, slowly constituting itself from a series of phonetic fragments, furnishes the verbal material for the piece. It is scored for mezzo-soprano, flute and clarinet, violin and cello, and piano; and it revolves around a cyclically repeated pitch set (ex. 5, below) which eventually breaks through to a climax and fades away. The pitch set is presented by the voice and by the piano which also (a) emphasises certain notes by sforzandi and (b) occasionally embroiders the set with the pitches excluded from it. Both pedals of the piano are permanently down, so as to provide a continuous and general resonance. This is fined down into selective resonances by the other four instruments which sustain or echo particular notes of the set, with the flute occasionally introducing independent melodic fragments.

When Berio decided to incorporate this piece into *Sinfonia* in the following year, he chose to maintain the original materials more or less intact, but added extra instruments that would be able to provide a subtle elaboration of each of the functions mentioned above. Thus vibraphone and, after a while, harp join the piano in following through the complete pitch set (though the harp also reinforces the flute's independent melodic fragments, and continually explores the piano's extraneous pitches). The selective resonances are enriched by the addition of three more female voices and by the expansion of the functions of the original violin and cello lines, now distributed among violins C, violas and cellos. (The interplay between violins C, at the back of the orchestra, and the violas and cellos at the front introduces a sense of aural perspective quite absent from the intimacy of the chamber version.) The lower strings also provide resonance for the lower extraneous pitches, as do the tenors and basses. Sforzandi on the piano are reinforced by saxophone and horn – though the latter also aids the resonance process. Thus apart from harp and horn, which have multiple (and complementary) roles, specific groups have specific harmonic functions. The full orchestral complement is reserved to underline the climax and final bars.

Structural properties of the pitch set

The pitch set consists of seven pitches, *f* a♭ *a* b♭ b♮ *c*♯ *d,* each used three times. It is divided into three sections by the consistent coupling of *f* and *a*. The first section uses only four pitches, the second all seven, and the third all seven plus repetitions of those pitches omitted from the first section. The properties of the resultant set are analysed in examples 5, 6 and 7. Recurrent pitch groupings are shown in example 5 by ⌐, with retrograded groupings indicated by ◡. The two three-note repetitions are particularly significant, since they establish the complementary whole-tone nuclei *f a b* and *d* b♭ *a* ♭. These act as centres of gravity within the resonance system, encouraging the ear to perceive the set as oscillating between two whole-tone areas.

Ex. 5

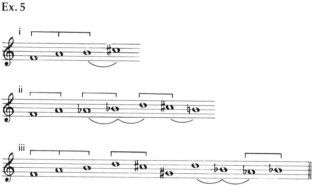

Ex. 6

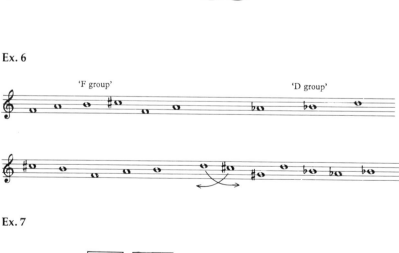

Ex. 7

The alternations between them are set out in example 6: the first discrete, the second overlapping. Each switch from one whole-tone area to the other is heralded by a semitone. The two semitones in section ii of the set (see ex. 5) focus attention on a further three-unit repetition, this time not of pitch but of interval content as *f a a♭* is followed by *b♭ d c♯*. This conjunction stands at the centre of a fourteen-pitch sequence richly structured by mutual pitch and interval relations, which is followed by a relatively 'loose' seven-pitch sequence, as in example 7.

We have thus at any rate three different ways of subdividing the twenty-one units of the pitch set according to different criteria: 4+7+10 (the triple return of *f a*); 6+3+5+2+5 (whole-tone areas); and 14+7 (pitch and interval repetitions). It is precisely because of its multi-faceted nature that the resultant set is capable of yielding so much musical substance when differently inflected at each repetition by the rhythmic set (see pp.26ff).

The pitch set in macrocosm

The pitch set is also divided up by a series of sforzandi which, during the course of four and a half cyclic repetitions, map onto it a macrocosmic version of itself. The pattern thus created is set out in example 8a. The end of each section of the macro-set is indicated by a vertical line, the end of the first cycle of that set by a double vertical line. Repetitions of individual pitches in the macro-set are placed in parentheses, interruptions (including the sforzando configuration in cycle **D**) in square brackets. Since cycles two to five begin at rehearsal letters **B–E**, I shall use these for reference, qualifying them with the numbers i–iii to indicate the three sections of the set.[1]

A simple displacement process generates the macro-structure. The two cycles start together on *f*, and the macro-set immediately dislocates itself by waiting for the *a* and *b* of **Aii**, the *c♯* from **Aiii**, and so forth. Naturally the two cycles will once again coincide at **Bii**, and it is an obvious logical possibility simply to repeat the initial dislocatory gesture whenever this occurs. This would create the hypothetical model shown in example 8b. As will be seen, by the start of the seventh cycle one has created a closed system which returns not to its starting-point, but to the start of the second cycle. While logically impeccable, this structure is musically somewhat over-extended, and provides for the contrast of groups of sforzandi only as and where the repetitions shown in example 5 permit them. By allowing the macro-set to run parallel with the normal set for several notes at a time in **Bii** and **Ciii**, Berio abbreviates this hypothetical model by two cycles, and at the same time provides a richer contrast between isolated sforzandi and groups of sforzandi.

[1] I label the first cycle **A** even though rehearsal letter **A** in the scores occurs at the position corresponding to the third note of **Aii** in this and subsequent diagrams. Rehearsal letter **E** in the *Sinfonia* score occurs one bar before the start of the fifth cycle.

Ex. 8

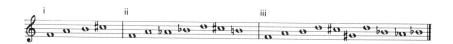

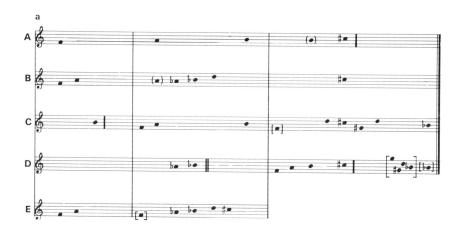

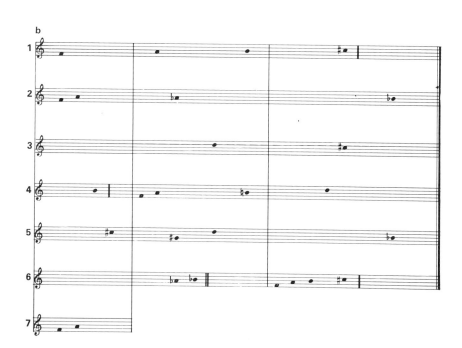

But these parallels are themselves subject to rigorous logical restraints. The first coincidence of macro-set and normal set occurs on the ab of **Bii**. It is a matter of indifference whether the parallelism is broken after the subsequent bb or d, since in either case the next coincidence will be in **Biii**; the choice is therefore made on the basis of rhythmic considerations, the d of **Bii** falling on a downbeat. To extend the parallelism to either the $c\sharp$ or the b would only modify the sforzando distribution pattern until the $g\sharp$ of **Ciii**, and would make the start of the third macro-group coincide with the start of **C**, thus creating a simplistic situation in which one section of the macro-set would correspond to each repetition of the basic set. To extend it any further would create an implausible imbalance in the sforzando distribution pattern, without providing any novel exit from its internal logic.[2]

A similar checkmate characterizes the second parallel group which starts on the d of **Ciii**, ushered in by the first break in the macro-set: the sforzando f at **C3** which by now constitutes an insistent and independent pedal. To break the coincidence after either $c\sharp$ or $g\sharp$ would merely generate an extra set-cycle before arriving at the situation of **Dii**. To extend it to bb or ab would again produce **Dii**; and on grounds of rhythm and excessive length Berio discards both alternatives. The extension to the final bb would produce a different distribution pattern up to the crucial and unavoidable $c\sharp$ of **Diii**, but is clearly too long; the extension to f would close the cycle.

This closure is, in any case, inescapable. The $c\sharp$ of **Diii** equals the $c\sharp$ of **Aiii**. If the pattern is not immediately broken, the cycle may continue indefinitely. Accordingly, on the first bb of **Diii**, the sforzandi leap to g, $g\sharp$, d and bb, and then focus on the second bb, marking it out as the note which, when it next recurs, will usher in the disruption of the normal set cycle and provoke a climax.

Climax and epilogue

The second bb of **Diii** also introduces a new feature: rapid crescendi and diminuendi; and these continue as the fifth cycle starts at **E**, confusing the clear-cut relation between normal structure and macro-structure. Indeed, the distinction between the two threatens to dissolve entirely when, in **Eii**, they reach the parallel to the first coincidence at **Bii**, discussed above. This is avoided only because neither ever completes **Eii**. Instead, after a long-held crescendo on the bb of **Eii**, the pitch set is disrupted and leaps to a high g, after which the melodic line falls away to a close. The resultant structure is shown in example 9, where the slightly more complex pattern used for the *Sinfonia* version is indicated by the additions in parentheses. Clearly, the melodic line after the climax consists of a synthesis of the retrogrades of the first four notes of ii, and the first five notes of iii. By adding a bb in the *Sinfonia* version to the alien ab

---

[2] The f and a of **Biii** would likewise lead to a further coincidence on the $g\sharp$ of **Ciii**; the subsequent b, d and $c\sharp$ would all generate line 5 of example 8b.

Ex. 9

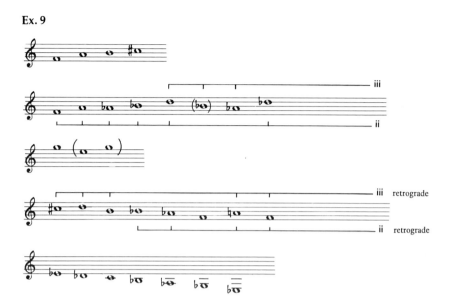

already existent in the chamber version Berio creates an analogous structure before the climax, integrating the pitches missing from the retrograde version of iii to be heard subsequently with the near-complete version of ii discussed above. Thus the missing Eiii nonetheless maintains a substantial presence.

At the end of the chamber setting, the voice part falls away to db, thus ending with an inversion of the omnipresent f–a relationship, and at the same time recalling the *punctum dolens* at which the set was shattered in Eii. In the *Sinfonia* version, the voices continue this process downward to form an eight-part chord (the interval order of a descending major scale down to the first bass, with the eb of the second bass balancing by inversion the major ninth between f and the climactic high g).

The rhythmic set

The twenty-one unit pitch set is combined with a twenty unit rhythmic set, so that with each repetition of the cycle the pitch set's internal relationships are inflected differently by the rhythmic set's displaced position. This is shown in example 10a, where the rhythmic values assigned to each note of the pitch set are set out as multiples of a quaver, with the variants introduced into the *Sinfonia* version noted below each line of the complete chamber version. Clearly, the rhythmic set is not a fixed entity like the pitch set, but gradually evolves. This is made immediately clear by the final bb of Aiii which, instead of starting the second statement of the rhythmic set with a further 8, elongates it to 17, which in turn becomes 7 when the third statement starts on the ab of Biii.

Such elongations apart – and their function will be discussed in due course – the rhythmic set is composed of eight different units

Ex. 10

'F group'　　　　　|'D group'　|'F group'　　　　　　|🗘|'D group'

i　　　　　　　ii　　　　　　　　　　iii

(musical staff with whole notes across sections i, ii, iii)

a

	i				ii							iii										
A	8	7	6	6	6	7	3	2	1	4	3		5	2	8	4	2	7	1	6	3 ‖	17
															3					8		
B	7	6	6	6	8	3	2	1	4	3	5		2	8	4	2	7	1	6	3 ‖	7	6
				4	6																	
C	6	6	6	8	2	3	1	4	3	5	2		8	4	2	7	1	6	3 ‖	7	6	6
D	6	6	8	3	2	1	4	3	3⅔	1½	6		4	2	5	1	6	3‖	1	6	6	12
									12								12					18
E	3	2	1	6	2	3	1	19⅔	1½													

b

A　　⌐‾‾‾‾‾‾|‾‾‾‾‾‾‾‾‾‾‾‾‾‾‾‾‾‾¬　　⌢‾‾‾‾‾‾‾‾‾

B　　⌐‾‾‾‾‾‾|‾‾¬　⌢‾‾¬　‾‾‾‾‾‾‾‾‾¬　⌢‾‾‾‾‾‾‾

C　　⌐‾‾‾‾‾‾|‾‾¬　⌢‾‾¬　‾‾‾‾‾‾‾‾‾¬　⌢‾‾‾‾‾‾‾

D　　⌐‾‾‾‾‾‾|‾‾¬　⌢‾‾¬　‾‾‾‾‾‾‾‾‾¬　⌢‾‾‾‾‾‾‾

⌐‾‾‾¬ = 'F group' dominance; ⌢ = 'D group' dominance as determined by upbeat patterns

ranging from one to eight quavers, and deployed so as to avoid repeated units within the sequence. This ensures that such aurally evident pitch repetitions as the *f a b* common to sections i and iii of the pitch set are always articulated in rhythmically contrasting ways. The structural properties of the rhythmic set are instead dictated by three partly related devices: (a) extreme durational contrasts, producing short 'upbeats' to long 'downbeats'; (b) sequences of durations that can be heard as implying metric rather than additive organisation (in which upbeat patterns play an important role); and (c) sequences of similar durations such as the 8:7:6:6:6:7 group which distinguishes the first whole-tone grouping in Ai and Aii from the second (articulated by a sharply contrasting 3:2:1).

Upbeat patterns

The oscillation between whole-tone groups that is so fundamental a feature of the pitch set is intimately bound up with the deployment of short–long durational patterns because of the implied accent that the longer note carries. To aid discussion, I shall refer to the two groups as *f* groups and *d* groups, reflecting the inversional relationship (*f a b* vs. *d bb ab*) that exists between them, as in example 6.

The first upbeat relationship of the rhythmic set is provided by the

1:4 relationship that first occurs in **Aii**.[3] Section ii of the pitch set has a *d*-group in the middle, flanked by *f*-groups; and in statement **A** the downbeat provided by this relationship falls on the first note of the second *f*-group. But as the 1:4 relationship shifts back one place in statements **Bii**, **Cii** and **Dii**, the downbeat now falls within the *d*-based group. Thus the *d*-group in **Aii**, although distinguished by shorter durations, is nonetheless subservient to the surrounding *f*-group, whereas in the other three statements it contains a rhythmic accent and therefore resists that dominance.

By contrast, the next upbeat relationship, the 2:8 of **Aiii**, under-goes no such modification of function, remaining within the *f*-based group spanning sections ii and iii of the pitch set throughout its three displacements (the last of which presents it in non-propor-tional diminution).

The only ambiguous area within the pitch set from the point of view of whole-tone oppositions is the overlap between the two groups provided by the pitch sequence *b d c♯ g♯* in iii; and the two remaining upbeat relations in the rhythmic series, provided by the rhythmic sequence 2:7:1:6, are used to resolve this ambiguity of harmonic orientation one way or the other. In statement **A**, the 2:7 relation gives the *c♯* an upbeat function, thus ensuring the dominance of the *d*-group from the first *d* of **Aiii**, through to the end of **A**, and reinforcing it with the 1:6 relation that follows. But in statement **B**, the *c♯* acquires a downbeat function, maintaining the dominance of the *f*-group up to that note, after which the 1:6 re-lation vigorously asserts the dominance of the *d*-group. Statement **C** is likewise clearly polarized, with both downbeats asserting the dominance of the *d*-group so that the dominance of the *f*-group can extend only to the *b* of **Ciii**, as in statement **A**. Naturally, state-ment **D** will revert to the pattern of statement **B**; only this time the polarities are exaggerated with 1:6 converting to 1:12 in the *Sinfonia* version, and with a new upbeat pattern being introduced by converting 7:6 of cycles **A–C** into 1:6 in order to give an equally emphatic downbeat to the *d*-group. These relationships are sum-marized in example 10b.

The growth of rhythmic stability

The upbeat patterns also serve to articulate areas of comparative metric coherence within an additive context. The first of these, the 3:2:1:4 in section ii of the pitch set,[4] may be scanned as a 6/8 pattern or indeed as a syncopated 3/4, which is how Berio notates it. The 6/8 interpretation is reinforced in statements **A** and **D** by articulating the last dotted crotchet of the previous duration as a vowel change, while in statement **B** the 3/4 interpretation is somewhat reinforced by the preceding crotchet-based durations. The implication of 3/4

---

[3] The 'downbeat' character of the 4 is further amplified by the implied 6/8 of the 3:2:1 sequence, discussed in the next section.

[4] In this context the 4 is relevant as an attack rather than a duration.

created by the permutation of this pattern in statement C will be discussed below.

The second metrically coherent sequence, the 2:8:4:2:7:1:6:3, is rather more complex.[5] After a crotchet upbeat, it may be scanned (and is notated) as an alternating pattern of 4/4 and 3/4. In the chamber version this pattern is maintained throughout the first three statements, but has its durational relationships (though not its upbeat patterns) modified in statement D, with metric consequences again to be discussed below.

As was noted above, the whole of the first f-group in A is unified by a group of similar durations, 8:7:6:6:6:7. This sequence is however subjected to immediate transformation, so that by its third repetition in statements B–C it has become 7:6:6:6:6:8. A crotchet additive basis now predominates over the original quaver basis; and dotted minims have now become more emphatically normative. The effect is compounded in C by the 2:3:1:4 permutation of the 3:2:1:4 sequence discussed above which follows, leading in turn to the crotchet-based second sequence, with only a minor additive dislocation in between. The ambiguities of statement A (additive quaver base vs. 6/8 metric base vs. metric alternation of 3/4 and 4/4), already under threat in statement B, have by now been ironed out into a norm of three crotchets, occasionally contradicted by groups of four or two. This final contradiction is to be eliminated in statements D and E, but not before a flurry of disruption as the 6/8 pattern reasserts itself, followed by a contradiction of the quaver additive basis in the $3\frac{2}{3}{:}1\frac{1}{3}$ relationship. The second metric sequence now follows, so modified as to scan entirely in 3/4 and, after a single bar of 2/4 (3:1), the music settles permanently into this metre until the precipitation of the climax.

An inordinately extended $b\flat$ at the end of statement A had ushered in the dislocation between pitch and rhythmic sets. A similarly extended $b\flat$ at the end of statement D now signals the collapse of the fixed relationship that has since then been maintained between them. The rhythmic series shifts not one place but three, relative to the pitch series, so that Ei is now articulated by the first metric sequence (3:2:1:6). This sequence is recapitulated for Eii in the same permutated version as Cii (2:3:1), thereby (a) breaking the rhythmic series, and (b) literally repeating an association of pitch and rhythm for the first time in the piece.[6] The music freezes once more onto $b\flat$, and breaks through to the climax – a 30-quaver long high g.[7]

The epilogue of the chamber version uses the rhythmic sequence

---

[5] Again, the final 3 is relevant only as an attack.

[6] With the exception of the dotted minims that will inevitably start both statements C and D.

[7] Its five dotted minims thus usurp the well-established pattern of four dotted minims in the rhythmic series; but in the *Sinfonia* version this also becomes five dotted minims in its last cycle.

4:6/ 7:2:4/ 7:6:18, here grouped to show possible derivations from the rhythmic set: 4:6 is a summary retrograde of the first metrically coherent sequence, 3:2:1:4;[8] 7:2:4 is a retrograde of part of the second metric sequence; and 7:6:18 is a summary version of the familiar 7:6:6:6:6 sequence. Inevitably, though, this interpretation is coloured by knowledge of comparable retrograde fragments in the pitch line at this point.

Rhythmic commentary in *Sinfonia*

In the cyclic repetitions leading up to the climax, only six units within the rhythmic set are modified in the *Sinfonia* version (see ex. 10a). But inasmuch as they are designed to alter the patterns of pitch–rhythm interaction discussed above, they consistute a first level of commentary. The first two groups of alterations are both designed to slow down the levelling out of rhythmic ambiguities discussed above. In Aiii, the substitution of 3 for 4 ensures that the second metric group will not achieve coherence until statement **B**, and that the point of maximum harmonic ambiguity in the pitch set is matched by equal rhythmic ambiguity. However, the substitution of 8 for 6 asserts the presence of 4/4 amid these additive dislocations. This will proliferate into an alternation of 3/4 and 4/4 in statements **B** and **C**, before finally resolving into a predominant 3/4 in **D**. The substitution of 4:6 for 6:8 in statement **B** mitigates the increasing emphatic chain of 6s, and at the same time provides a summary retrograde of the 3:2:1:4 that follows, thereby reinforcing, by more extensive preparation, the upbeat pattern in that sequence, with its important harmonic implications discussed above. The other group of modifications, in Diii, is exclusively concerned with emphasising pre-established harmonic polarities: the 12 on the $c\sharp$ firmly resolving any suggestion of ambiguity in the pitch set, and the final $b\flat$ being raised to 18 by way of compensation.

The epilogue of the *Sinfonia* version offers a substantially altered sequence – 4:6:8:1⅓:3⅔:8:7:6. The 4:6:8 could be construed as an extension of the same sequence in the chamber version;[9] the 1⅓:3⅔ retrogrades the configuration from **Dii** which, in its expanded form at **Eii**, ushers in the climax; and 8:7:6 simply recapitulates the opening sequence.

Parallel processes in rhythm and pitch

Thus within the two fixed systems of this piece analogous processes operate. Both derive their dynamism from internal oppositions either between levels of structure (pitch set vs. macro-set, quaver vs. crotchet additive unit), or between different types of organisation (additive vs. metric, triple vs. quadruple). Both are obliged to break through to a climax once these oppositions are played out, lest they should lapse into a monolithic and logically unending gyre of

[8] A relationship clarified in the *Sinfonia* version: see below.
[9] Save that in the *Sinfonia* version the third unit should no longer be 8 but 6.

continuous sforzando statements of the pitch set in 3/4. In each case the moment at which oppositions become reconciled is instantly countered by a flouting of the system (the pitch macro-structure in Diii, the rhythmic structure in Ei) and a build-up towards a climax. Once the climax is spent, predominantly retrograded fragments from both series provide an epilogue.

Selective resonance

The interactions of pitch and rhythmic sets produce a single, highly structured melodic line which is subjected to comparatively little modification as it is transferred from the chamber version to the *Sinfonia* version. But within each note is heard a series of echo attacks from the sustaining instruments and, in *Sinfonia*, the other high voices. Sometimes these anticipate the pitches of the main line; almost invariably they hold each note of that line over into the next – either to create a momentary harmonic blur, or else to sustain that note through one or several subsequent notes. The aggregate rhythm of these attacks[10] does not appear to be subject to a system,[11] but the harmonic process that they create is the major generator of large-scale form in both versions. It consists, quite simply, in a gradual increase of harmonic density achieved by a progress from momentary blurs as the general norm to sustained notes as the general norm. The process is more rapid and more marked in the *Sinfonia* version (see below, p.34).

In the early stages of this process, and before the harmonic field has been complicated by the frequent incursion of alien pitches, the result of selective resonance is to focus the ear on the alternation between whole-tone groupings discussed above. However, on occasion Berio enriches his resources by holding the outer note from each group over into the opposite group. This gesture is particularly characteristic of statement **B** of the pitch cycle in the chamber version – though the use of an *f* pedal is extended through much of the subsequent material in *Sinfonia* – and in each case it produces a fleeting tonal reference. An *f* pedal sounded below the *ab bb d* group evokes the second inversion of a dominant seventh chord on *bb*, as

[10] They are complicated further by internal rhythms within the main vocal line as it changes vowel or introduces a jaw tremolo within the note. The vocal line also deploys acciaccaturas, some of which effect temporary permutations of the pitch set.

[11] Berio himself thinks that he can recall some sort of systematic starting point for their organisation, so others may well care to correct me. In the chamber version there are, however, remnants of a system governing the number of notes from the twenty-one pitch set played by each of the four sustaining instruments. In statement **A** the flute plays eighteen, clarinet, violin and cello fourteen. In statement **C** all play fourteen save the cello, which plays eleven. In statement **D** all play eleven save the cello, which plays nine. This modest game with a number series serves to systematize the increased number of pitches held over to consolidate the central melody's harmonic implications, as a result of which each instrument can play fewer notes of the series. But it is quite lost sight of in statement **B** (flute fifteen, clarinet twelve, violin sixteen, cello eleven), and in any case disappears within the more complex circumstances of *Sinfonia*.

in the final notes of **Biii**, reproduced in example 11a in rough proportional notation. Similarly, a *d* sustained above the opposite group of *f a b c♯* gives a momentary hint of *d* minor – an impression reinforced when *f* is sustained throughout. Example 11b outlines an instance of this: **Bi** and the first three notes of **Bii**. In both these examples the total harmonic impression is a slightly more complex experience, due to the embroidery of extraneous pitches supplied by the piano.

Ex. 11

Independent melodic lines

All the features so far discussed either fall within, or are generated by the central melodic line. But from time to time the flute, supported by the harp, introduces its own melodic fragments based on the pitch repertoire set out in example 12. Clearly, this incorporates the *d*-based whole-tone group, plus a complementary *c* and an alien *c♯* that mirrors the *c♯*–*d* coupling in the pitch set. As might be expected, the flute entries therefore tend to underline the appearance of the *d*-group within the set – at first as a heterophonic ornament to the vocal line, but thereafter as an independent voice.

Ex. 12

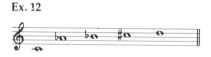

In statements **A** to **C**, it always appears in conjunction with the *d*-group of section ii of the set; in statement **A** it also occurs both at the start and the end of the *d*-group in section iii – while in statement **B** it occurs only at the start, and in statement **C** only at the end. In this last instance similar materials are heard for the first time on the clarinet; and the flute in echoing it spills over into alien territory: the *f*-group at the start of statement **D**. The flute now takes over from the piano part the high *g* that is to dominate the music increasingly in preparation for the climax. It pursues an independent path until **Diii** when, abandoning its established pitch repertoire, it follows the vocal line – though breaking free from it to insist upon the high *g* to which the voice, too, must eventually come.

As the flute begins to herald one feature of the climax at **D**, the violas (cello in the chamber version) hint at another. Picking up the flute's low *c* they establish another independent line which rises by degrees to *f*, where it blends into the vocal line. No more is heard of this until the long *b♭* that precedes the climax, when all the free parts rise in a flurry of similar lines beneath the flute's held *g*, saturating the chromatic space from the *g♯* below.

Pitches outside the set

In the chamber version of *O King*, the five notes excluded from the set are assigned to the piano, save for the *c* incorporated into the flute's pitch repertoire. Four of them, *e♭*, *g*, *c* and *e*, are disposed symmetrically around the gamut of the pitch set, with the *f♯* establishing a further downward extension, as shown on the left-hand side of example 13. They remain in these positions throughout statements **A** and **B**, but from statement **C** onwards begin to attain greater mobility, as shown by the black note-heads in example 13. However, a new octave placement for a pitch class does not preclude the recurrence of previous placements, so that throughout statement **C** we find an alternation between *e♭* and *f♯* in both extreme registers. Octave placements of *e♭*, *e* and *f♯* become even more fluid in statement **D**, though the *f♯* in parentheses occurs only in the *Sinfonia* version. However, *c* and *g* remain fixed throughout – the latter in preparation for the climax, of which it is the focus.

Ex. 13

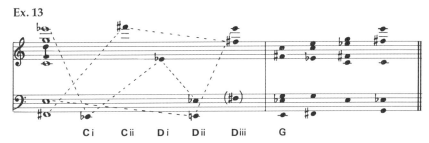

Although initially employed as whole-tone complements to the pitch set's two harmonic areas (so that *c* and *e* in **Aii** usher in the first *d*-group, *e♭* the second *f*-group, etc.), these pitches soon combine freely, forming a network of extraneous pitches around the harmonic core of the pitch set. But in *Sinfonia* Berio assigns a more complex role to the lower pitches, initially *c*, *e* and *f♯*, by having them sung or played by sustaining instruments, so that they interact with the harmonic projections of the pitch set. Since the consequences of this depend in part upon modifications in the resonance system, the two are best considered together in the next section.

Immediately after the climax, as all voices converge upon the high *g*, a new independent bass line emerges whose pitches – *c b♭ a♭* repeated, and then *c♯ b a* repeated – underline the opposition between whole-tone areas that has lain at the heart of the piece (resolving it, by interaction with the vocal line, in favour of the *f* whole-tone scale). Above this, the chamber version rearranges the alien pitches in a series of chords, shown on the right-hand side of example 13, that finally settle into an 'inversion' of the original chord around its central *c*. In the *Sinfonia* version these are thickened into twelve-note chords reminiscent of those of the first movement in interval distribution, and hinting at the massive, saturated blocks that are to play so formidable a part in the third movement.

Harmonic commentary upon the chamber version in *Sinfonia*

The greater harmonic density of the *Sinfonia* version of *O King* has already been noted. This is in part due to the more persistent use of pedals. Thus, whereas in the chamber version an f pedal does not become an important factor until **Biii**, and retires into relative insignificance from **Ciii** on, in *Sinfonia* it is a persistent presence from the start of statement **B** through to the climax. Furthermore, in both **Dii** and **Diii** it is expanded to produce a recurrent harmonic core, $f\,ab\,bb$, around which the dense and constantly shifting harmony can revolve. Since the earlier whole-tone and quasi-tonal implications are by now completely obliterated, these recurrent pedals act as an important stabilising influence.

But from the start the *Sinfonia* version has a richer harmonic texture due to the presence of sustained pitches from outside the set. The recurring presence of c and e in the low strings and basses is a crucial factor in this respect. Their first two appearances, in **Aii** and **Aiii**, merely give added resonance to the original piano part. But when they are introduced beneath the sustained f and d that initiate both **Bi** and **Bii**, they abolish the bare simplicity of the chamber version, as they do when added, along with a low $f\sharp$, to the sustained f and $c\sharp$ of **Bii**.

This corruption of simple consonance continues throughout statement **C**. Thus the a of **Ci** whose consonance with a sustained f was originally troubled only by a quiet resonance of e and $f\sharp$ from the piano now has that resonance amplified; and a sustained eb from double basses ensures that overtones will cloud the clarity of the f–$c\sharp$ and f–a relationships that start **Bii**. A tritone relationship is likewise invaded with the final ab of **Ciii** – originally sounding only with a sustained d, but now with the familiar $c\ e$ and $f\sharp$ to cloud matters in the bass. The pitches c and e return in the latter part of **Diii** to further densen a texture already far richer than the original because of the sustained f, ab and bb discussed above.

By thickening out the harmonies in this way, Berio establishes a greater measure of harmonic identity between 'O King', and the first, fourth and fifth movements of *Sinfonia* – particularly the fourth, where chords of alternating thirds and seconds over wider-spaced bass notes are a fundamental feature. (Compare, for instance, **Aii** in 'O King' with the final chords of the first two progressions in the fourth movement.) But he also establishes an important harmonic progression from the deliberately simple, third-based chords of the first movement, through the more sophisticated harmonic flux around a single melodic line of the second movement to the extremely rich harmonic vocabulary of the third movement.

The text and its structural potential

Although phonetic materials derived from the text were used in the first movement to help maintain a precarious balance between sound and sense, only the simplest of structural relations were established between them (the front–back opposition of 'tktktktk' as the voices disappear, for instance). But here the gradual constitution of 'O Martin Luther King' from its phonetic constituents demands a more analytical approach. Berio is much helped in this by the structured nature of the International Phonetic Alphabet, which offers a system based upon the changing positions of the mobile speech organs. The very elegance and concision of this 'postural' typology, which was synthesized from the pre-war work of Daniel Jones and other members of the International Phonetic Association, have made it an object of some controversy amongst phoneticians since its publication in 1949.[12] But it is precisely these qualities that make the system useful and stimulating for a musician. For instance, the alphabet distinguishes a set of 'cardinal vowels' governed by two factors: where in the mouth the vowel is sounded (i.e. front vs. back), and whether the mouth is opened or partly closed. These are combined to produce the matrix set out in example 14.[13] Similar oppositions can be used to classify consonants, though here three factors must be considered: (a) front vs. back (upon which the I.P.A. bases its own classification to the exclusion of other factors[14]); (b) total stoppage of the airflow, followed by release (plosives) vs. unhindered airflow (nasals and laterals), with the vibrating rolls and fricatives occupying a mid-point; (c) voiced vs. unvoiced.

Ex. 14

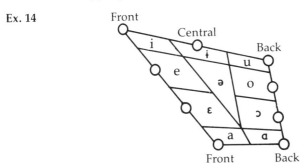

If we now examine the phonetic constituents of 'O Martin Luther King' in the light of these distinctions, their structural potential becomes obvious. The vowels [o] [a] [i] [u] [ʒ][15] [i] can be arranged so as to form a circular sequence around the mouth from front closed, through front open and back closed – [i] [ʒ] [a] [o] [u] [i] – and it is thus that they are first presented. This anticlockwise motion around example 14 is then maintained by permutating the sequence into two triangular sequences: [o] [i] [ʒ] and [a] [u] [i]. The purpose of this begins to become clear in the next sequence, where a clock-

---

[12] See, for instance, John Laver's critique in Lyons ed. 1970, pp.55–7.

[13] Reproduced from International Phonetic Association 1949, p.6. The peculiar shape of this figure is due to the maximal front–back opposition obtained with a closed mouth.

[14] See International Phonetic Association 1949, p.10.

[15] Berio's [ʒ] equals the [ɛ] of the International Phonetic Association and represents the vowel of /ther/.

wise triangle [o] [a] [i] is juxtaposed with an anticlockwise triangle [ʒ] [u] [i]. The first of these presents the vowels as in the text; and accordingly Berio produces a fourth sequence which permutates the second triangle so as to produce the complete correct order. These games are summarized in example 15.[16]

Ex. 15

The correct order of vowels having been established, Berio starts to add consonants. These too are arranged according to their phonetic characteristics. Of the six consonants used structurally, three are voiced,[17] and three unvoiced. Of the three voiced consonants two are nasal (the velar [ŋ] that ends 'King' and the bilabial [m]) and one lateral (the alveolar [l]). Of the unvoiced consonants two are plosive (the velar [k] and the dental [t]) and one fricative (the dental [θ] representing the /th/ of 'Luther'). The two voiced nasals and the two unvoiced plosives each establish a front–back opposition, though it is only the former, between opening and closing consonants, that is put to structural use.

The gradual addition of consonants proceeds from the vowel-like voiced consonants to the more disruptive, unvoiced ones. Statement A of the pitch series is taken up entirely with the ordering of vowels. Statement B introduces the nasal opposites [ŋ] and [m], and these are joined in statement C by [l]. From statement D, however, the two versions part company. The chamber version continues with vowels and voiced consonants, witholding the first unvoiced consonant, [k], until just before E. It then adds [θ] at the climax, and allows [t] only a single appearance in the full version of the text sung in the epilogue. Both voiced and unvoiced consonant pairs are thus introduced in the order from back to front. In *Sinfonia*, on the other hand, it is [t] that is introduced first, and it appears soon after the start of statement D. [θ] is introduced in the middle of D, and [k] at the same place as in the chamber version. The order of introduction of the unvoiced consonants is thus reversed.

[16] Games with vowel rotation, normally triangular, can also be found in *Sequenza III*. They bring into play a set of 'secondary cardinal vowels' for which a diagram analogous to example 14 can be found on p.6 of International Phonetic Association 1949. Comparison between those diagrams and the first system of p.2 in the score will reveal a fairly complex example (provided that the vowels from word fragments are phonetically transcribed).

[17] A fourth voiced consonant, the nasal alveolar [n], occurs in the text; but it is too close to [ŋ] to be used distinctively in Berio's structural games. It therefore appears only when he introduces the [t] with which it is associated. It is only in the *Sinfonia* version that a distinction is made between /ma/ and 'Mar' after D, thereby acknowledging the sounded [r] of American pronunciation.

Permutation and troping

As far as the chamber version is concerned, the pattern that results from this gradual accumulation of phonetic constituents is a relatively simple one, varied only by the alternation between adjacent vowels or syllables of the text. It is set out in example 16, where each element that cannot be accommodated on the same line starts a new one.[18] What first strikes the eye is Berio's opening sequence of permutations which are as coherent from the point of view of text order as they are from that of vowel rotation. Initially the vowel chain forms a pattern of one step back (noted by ╱), three steps forward.[19] The next group of six then forms two chains of two steps forward (noted by ⌢). The third group of six combines ⌢ and ╱ to permutate its second half.

Once the correct vowel sequence has been established, the permutations that follow are dictated by two considerations. In the first place there would appear to be the relics, only partly obliterated, of a simple system determining the number of vowels or syllables to be sung within each statement of the pitch set. In statement **A** there are twenty-seven, in statement **B** eighteen, in statement **C** nine,[20] in statement **D** seventeen (presumably eighteen in the original groundplan), and from **E** to the climax nine. This would give an underlying scheme of 9×9 (and indeed, if one includes the otherwise mysterious [ø] of statement **C**, the overall number is still adhered to). In addition, the permutations serve to build towards the introduction of new consonants in all cases save /ther/. As might be expected, Berio selects for his two principal alternations the strongest opposites contained within the normal order of the text: the front–back closed 'i/u', and the even stronger back open/front closed 'a/i'.

The thinning-out of verbal events in the middle of the chamber version produced extended melismas; and these offered Berio the opportunity for elaboration when he came to write the *Sinfonia* version. He responded with phonetic tropes. Initially these reflect the systematic permutations of the opening, so that after the complete text sequence at the start of statement **C** (complicated only by the insertion of an extra [u]) phonemes jump backwards by twos – '[ŋ] lu [a]' – and then by ones – '[ŋ] [ʒ] lu'. But they become rather more maverick by statement **D** – as well they might, for during this statement the other seven voices, which up to now have echoed the first soprano's materials faithfully, become infected by the general move towards proliferation, and proceed to trope her line. The resultant phonetic *mêlée* produces a richer, more disordered verbal texture that parallels the steady increase in harmonic density.

---

[18] This method of exposition is borrowed from Ruwet 1972, pp.100ff.

[19] Provided, that is, that the ambiguous [i]s are resolved as shown.

[20] If the [o] straddling statements **B** and **C** is counted as part of **B**, and the [ø] that occurs after the next [o] is taken simply as an inflection of that vowel.

Ex. 16

O   Mar - tin   Lu - ther   King

4
'In ruhig fliessender Bewegung'

The second movement of *Sinfonia*, like the *Chemins*, had been the result of reopening a set of creative questions that were temporarily closed. But in the third movement Berio undertook a more daring and problematic project: that of building fresh layers of material not out of the residue of his own past compositional decisions, but around a work by another composer. He had long admired and studied Mahler's music, finding in its vivid but ironic eclecticism a congenial example for his own work; and his choice accordingly fell on the scherzo from Mahler's Second Symphony.[1] But its diatonic language posed a complex technical problem. For if Berio had sought to generate layers of commentary from the Mahler text itself he would have had to subject it to extensive transformation. If instead he had relied entirely upon his own harmonic vocabulary the gap between text and commentary would have been too great. So he opted for materials that establish a wide harmonic range – many of them quotations from other composers' work. Thus against Mahler's predominant diatonicism are set the more sumptuous harmonies of Ravel, Strauss and Debussy, the atonality of the second Viennese school, and massive, chromatically saturated orchestral clusters.[2] Merely to superpose these leaving the original intact, as in the previous movement, would clearly make for a cloying density of texture – as well as demanding gargantuan forces. Berio therefore blocked out ever greater amounts of the original material, at first so as to provide room for the various commentary materials, but later as an autonomous process that leaves only a skeleton of Mahlerian fragments. It is this incremental obliteration that provides the large-scale shape of the movement.

---

[1] Previously Berio had considered using the second movement of the symphony and even the final three movements of Beethoven's Op.131 as vehicles for a similar exercise. See Berio 1985, pp.107–8.

[2] The actual choice of materials was in part a matter of circumstance. Berio wrote the movement while on holiday in Sicily, and therefore relied upon the few scores that he had with him, those that happened to be available from Catania public library, and his own memory in order to establish a suitable range.

From sermon to scherzo

The movement from Mahler's Second Symphony chosen by Berio as a vehicle for this experiment was in several respects a peculiarly suitable starting-point. In the first place it, too, was the product of elaboration from a pre-established musical text. Although Mahler's song *Des Antonius von Padua Fischpredigt* and its expansion into the scherzo of the Second Symphony both reached completion at roughly the same time in the summer of 1893,[3] it is clear from Mahler's comments to Natalie Bauer-Lechner concerning the genesis of the scherzo that it must have been preceded by a more or less complete draft of the song.[4] The song in question sets an ironic text from the *Des Knaben Wunderhorn*, a collection of 'old German songs', compiled by Achim von Arnim and Clemens Brentano and published in two volumes of 1806 and 1808 with a dedication to Goethe. It narrates how, for lack of a congregation, St Anthony goes to preach to the fishes who are listed – each with their more or less venial characteristics – as they rise to the surface to listen in admiration. But, after enjoying a moment's edification, each returns refreshed to its favourite indulgence. The association between this song-text and the music of the scherzo gives rise to a number of semantic games within Berio's movement, to be discussed below (pp.53ff). But for the moment our concern must be with the musical form that Mahler moulds around it. In the song this is a simple ternary structure, with a first section consistently focused upon *c* minor, answered by *c* major, a middle section that similarly never moves far from the ambit of *f* major, and finally a reworking of the first section, incorporating somewhat more devious tonal sallies as the fish disperse to their sinful pursuits.

The elaboration of so concise a structure into an orchestral scherzo involves considerable expansion. The correlation is direct until the end of the middle section of the song,[5] which forms a first 'trio' within this orchestral context. Materials from the final section of the song are incorporated into the second reprise[6] and at the end,[7] but otherwise the orchestral version introduces new materials or reworks previously stated ones. Thus the first trio in *f* is followed by a first reprise of the scherzo in the tonic, allowing a slightly richer range of temporary modulations (b.149–89). There then follows a substantial new section – to be referred to, slightly incongruously in view of its emphatic character, as Trio II (b.190–347). This dramatizes the rather bland contrast previously established between *c* and

---

[3] See Mitchell 1975. pp.137–8.

[4] Indeed, Mahler's observation that 'Without knowing at first where it's leading, you find yourself pushed further and further beyond the bounds of the original form, whose potentialities lay hidden within it like the plant within the seed' (Bauer-Lechner 1980, p.32) would, but for its implications of diachronic expansion, provide an excellent summary of Berio's approach to musical commentary.

[5] b.2–133 of the song = b.6–137 of the scherzo.

[6] b.140–58 of the song, transposed up a fourth = b.387–406 of the scherzo.

[7] b.171–end of the song = b.555–end of the scherzo.

f by brusque upward steps from *c* major through *d* major to *e* major. A return to *c* major leads back into a second reprise of the scherzo materials (b.348–406). This is followed by a combined reprise of materials from Trio I (b.407–40) and Trio II (b.441–543), with the latter moving to a massive climax represented by a chord of *b♭* minor over a *c* pedal (b.465) whose programmatic significance will be discussed on p.54. There follows the final reprise of the scherzo materials, blending back into the final bars of the song, as noted above.[8]

It should however be emphasised that these relationships are confined purely to matters of pitch and rhythm. Since the first orchestral draft of the scherzo was completed only eight days after the piano score of the song,[9] and since the 'meticulous' instrumental indications of the latter were fleshed out into an orchestral score of the song three weeks later,[10] there is clearly no justification for regarding the integrated, post-Wagnerian orchestral palette of the scherzo as being a commentary or elaboration upon the simpler, 'choral' use of chamber orchestra resources in the song. On the contrary, the two versions would appear to offer a remarkable example of closely related melodic, harmonic and rhythmic materials projected, more or less concurrently, into two contrasting sound-worlds.[11]

Texts for a sermon

But Mahler's scherzo provides a further and rather more curious precedent for Berio's experiment. The idea of using materials from other composers' works as a means of blocking out the Mahler text is complemented by Mahler's own use – conscious or unconscious – of alien materials in his *Fischpredigt*. These analogies are set out in example 17. The parallel between b.44–52 of the Mahler and the trio from Bruckner's Fourth Symphony is fairly straightforward, save that Mahler does not employ Bruckner's surprise modulation for the last two bars of the passage and he resolves the dominant harmonies of the third bar onto tonic harmony in the fourth. However, the similarity to Beethoven's trio does not end merely with the thematic material,[12] for the overall structure of the central section of the *Fischpredigt* (and therefore of Trio I of the scherzo) also shows close affinities with Beethoven's model. In both cases the eight-bar phrase quoted is repeated once, with some textural variation, followed by two two-bar phrases that develop their respective

---

[8] For a a more thorough discussion of relations between song and scherzo, see Tibbe 1971, pp.50–58.

[9] On 16th and 8th July 1893 respectively; see Mitchell 1975, pp.137–8.

[10] Finished on 1st August 1893; see Mitchell, *loc. cit.*

[11] A simple but extended example may be had by comparing b.40–59 of the song with b.44–63 of the scherzo; the interested reader will find many other more detailed contrasts elsewhere in the two scores.

[12] Though this, too, is reworked by altering the final modulation and by converting Beethoven's dominant seventh in the third bar to a subdominant.

Ex. 17

Bruckner, Fourth Symphony, Trio, and Mahler b.44-52

Beethoven, Violin Sonata Op. 96, Trio, and Mahler b.104-12

Schumann, *Das ist ein Flöten und Geigen*, Dichterliebe, No. 9, final bars, and Mahler final bars

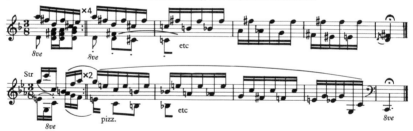

opening gestures to provide some tonal and harmonic variety, followed by a reprise of the original phrase which is, however, extended – in the Beethoven by extensive canonic repetitions based on the first half of the phrase, in the Mahler by developing a repetition of the second half of the phrase. The allusion to the final gesture from Schumann's 'Das ist ein Flöten und Geigen' at the end of both song and scherzo is straightforward from a musical point of view. Its possible programmatic significance will be discussed below on p.54.[13]

[13] The Schumann quotation is noted and discussed in Tibbe 1971, pp.58–9, where she, too, underlines its congruence with the programme of the symphonic scherzo. The Bruckner quotation is noted in Altmann 1977, pp.19–20, though without discussion of its significance. Neither of these authors discusses the Beethoven quotation.

Whether or not these should be regarded as conscious quotations is difficult to determine. Despite Mahler's notorious delight in incongruous stylistic juxtapositions, there would appear to be little evidence in the current literature for the deliberate use of quotation elsewhere in his works. And his allegiance to a largely diatonic idiom inevitably encouraged parallels with the earlier nineteenth-century repertoire – though parallels as substantial as those discussed above can hardly be attributed to chance. Furthermore, Mahler was not unduly reticent in commenting on his own work, and while he does indeed acknowledge the influence of popular music from his Bohemian childhood in the *Fischpredigt*,[14] he makes no direct acknowledgement of these other influences.

On the other hand, since Mahler was well acquainted with all three works in question it seems unlikely that the parallels should have entirely escaped him. Indeed, there is some flimsy but tempting evidence to support the view that they were entirely deliberate. In another discussion of the *Fischpredigt* with Natalie Bauer-Lechner, Mahler is reported as saying: 'St Anthony preaches to the fishes; his words are immediately translated into their thoroughly tipsy-sounding language (in the clarinet)'.[15] The clarinet entry in question could be either that at b.16 of the song (b.20 of the scherzo) or that following the Bruckner quotation at b.48 of the song (b.52 of the scherzo). If the latter is indeed the case, then we have a delightfully wicked parallel between St Anthony and the similarly naive but devout Anton Bruckner. Further hints at hidden meaning are proffered as Mahler describes the recalcitrant fishes returning to their indulgences: 'Not one of them is one iota the wiser for it, even though the Saint has performed for them! But only a few people will understand my satire on mankind.'[16] Could that satire include the deliberate use of 'the tootling of the Bohemian pipers'[17] as a counter-subject to Beethoven? And might not a parable on that permanent Mahlerian obsession, the philistinism of his bourgeois public, well end with the final bars of a song whose last two lines run 'da-zwischen schluchzen und stöhnen die lieblichen Engelein'?[18]

Obliteration as form

Mahler's groundplan infuses the balanced, sectional design of a scherzo and two trios with a measure of dynamic unity by allowing the second of the trios such comparatively weighty materials that, when recapitulated along with those of Trio I, they carry the movement through to a unifying dramatic climax. Berio imposes upon this succession of discrete sections a single process of incremental obliteration that has already achieved fairly drastic form by Trio II –

[14] Bauer-Lechner 1980, p.33.
[15] Bauer-Lechner 1980, p.32.
[16] Bauer-Lechner 1980, p.33.
[17] *Ibid*.
[18] 'Amidst all this, the lovely angels sob and sigh.'

so that thereafter the continued presence of the Mahler is principally established by the sudden re-emergence of such major rhetorical gestures as the transitions between sections, the climax and the final bars. This process is summarized in example 18, which distinguishes five different levels of 'presence' of the original text (whose formal outlines are summarized beneath):

(i) conservation of the melodic and harmonic substance of Mahler's scherzo;

(ii) conservation of single – usually melodic – lines only;

(iii) conservation of fragments of Mahler's text, which appear in the same position relative to the metric framework that they occupied in the original. When that is not the case, as between **R** and **S**, **U** and **V**, or **W** and **X**, this is shown by a line oscillating between this level and level (v);

(iv) obliteration of the Mahler text while retaining its metric framework, so that when it does reappear, the same number of bars have elapsed as would have passed in the original;

(v) obliteration of text and metric framework. Although this occurs frequently from **P** onwards, the addition and subtraction of bars balance each other to a reasonable degree – with the result that Berio's movement, from the point at which it engages with the Mahler scherzo (b.7) to the end, lasts only eighteen bars more than its model.

(D) indicates distortions imposed upon the Mahler without interrupting its continuity, to be discussed below on p.47.

Above the graph are summarized the major features used to block out Mahler's original: chromatically saturated clusters (Cl), chromatic scales (Sc), quotation (Qu) and reduction of the Mahler to a few skeletal features (R) – when this process is used autonomously, and not merely to make space for one of the other three. Quotations are noted in this outline only where they completely block out Mahler's text: the many instances of dialogue between quotations and Mahler will be discussed below (p.48), and analysed instance by instance on pp.57ff. Although before **H** superposed clusters and scales perform a similar function of dialogue with Mahler's text, they have nonetheless been noted in brackets so as to show their localised occurrence.

On the whole, the application of these devices is regulated by individual features of the Mahler text rather than by some autonomous, self-regulating system. But it will be clear from example 18 that their distribution also helps to shape the form of the movement. Apart from a brief appearance at **T** as the quotation from Wozzeck escalates in density, the massive orchestral clusters are used exclusively to block out Mahler's upward tonal steps in Trio II and in the reprise of the same material at **Y**. Reduction gradually increases in importance, so that from the trio reprise onwards its gaunt textures establish a norm that contrasts sharply with the hectic abundance of earlier sections. Chromatic scales are at best

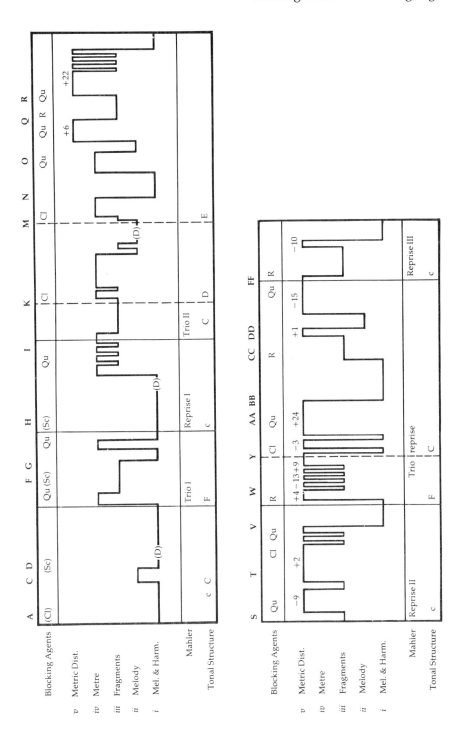

Ex. 18

only a comparatively minor resource, but their disappearance after the first reprise, recurring only as an integral part of the *Wozzeck* quotation at **S**, serves as a modest structural marker.

Although Berio has imposed a linear if vacillating process of obliteration upon an originally sectional conception, he does respect the rough contours of Mahler's dramatic structure. He thus conserves – indeed amplifies – the first part of Trio II as a high-point of tension, preparing it with a lengthy quotation from Stravinsky's *Le Sacre du printemps* before **I**, and allowing its energy to reverberate through to the combined Ravel–Strauss quotation at **O**. Although a comparatively contained dramatic crisis is inserted at **T**, prepared by the *Wozzeck* quotation, Berio otherwise follows Mahler in restraining his forces until the reprise of the Trio II material. Here, however, metric distortion begins to play an important role in reworking the dramatic structure, for whereas the outburst at **Y** should, according to the Mahlerian model, lead straight into the climax (cf. Mahler, b.441ff), Berio inserts a sudden quiet flashback to previously heard materials from *La Mer*. Similarly after the climax, where Mahler allows his nightmare vision to continue with quiet but undimmed energy for a considerable period, Berio cuts the overall length to compensate for his earlier insertion, and collapses the music immediately into a bleak, static texture whose suppressed tensions are only occasionally allowed to erupt.

Reduction and distortion

Reduction of Mahler's text to a few skeletal features is only slowly allowed to emerge as an autonomous feature. In a passage such as E12–F9 the snatches of Mahler have no perceptual priority over the various other quotation fragments and chromatic scales. By I7–**K** and L4–**M**, although fragments from other sources are still the dominant feature, the paring down of Mahler's texture has begun to assert itself more prominently. Particularly characteristic is the retaining of flute and piccolo high *c*s as a fixed point of reference against which a variety of fragments are projected. At **Q** the process finally moves to the foreground, isolating the oscillating trumpets of Mahler b.320 from their context, and using them to set in relief fragments of Mahlerian melody. The device is expanded upon at **V6**, where an ostinato is built up from a combination of Mahler b.433–4 (horns) and b.407 (cello) along with an oscillating woodwind figure that is a legacy from previous pages, all serving as a background to distorted fragments of Mahler and Hindemith. At **CC** (Mahler b.481) Berio amplifies upon his treatment of Mahler at I7, retaining the upper woodwind pedal but resisting the opportunity that Mahler offers for a further set of oscillations. In the final example at **FF**, it is only the grelots' ostinato that provides a fixed point of reference for the melodic fragments – though that too disintegrates as the movement closes.

Just as Mahler's text is constantly subject to some measure of reduction, so too his instrumentation is frequently modified. In part this is merely a further consequence of the need to make room for other events, but it is also used to break up the even flow of Mahler's lines. This may be achieved by the subtle changes of timbre and acoustic direction that come from tossing a melody from one string group to another as at A23,[19] or by etching in fragments of a line in another part as at N (Mahler b.272), where the original second violin countermelody is tossed from instrument to instrument through an enormously enriched string texture, doubled fragmentarily by saxophone and voices. Only occasionally does a radical rescoring come to the forefront of aural attention, but L4–M (Mahler b.235–57) is a remarkably sustained example of the device. Details of this and the many other minor examples will be found in the commentary (pp.57ff).

There is one other, very much more localized transformation to which Mahler's text is subjected: that of melodic distortion. Three different processes are used. The first is the expansion of a melodic line into a heterophony by simultaneous rhythmic distortion. This appears briefly at D4, but is more expansively treated from H onwards, where its scope is widened by instructing the singers to imitate – presumably in delayed and distorted form – given instrumental lines. In contrast to the blurry conservation of melodic shapes ensured by this device, the wide-ranging octave displacement that briefly follows upon its first appearance at D9 offers a capital opportunity for disguise. This is exploited to the full by piano and solo violin from W on. The developed use of heterophony at H also explores a mode of distortion peculiar to the keyboards: that of apparently random octave doublings. Here they are mainly confined to the right hands, while the left juggle with the bass part from the Mahler abandoned by the cellos. But the device recurs in purer form in the reorchestrated passage at L, with each keyboard elaborating upon one melodic line.

Quotation

The harmonic gamut established by the Mahler in its original and distorted forms is substantially amplified by the overlaid quotations. The majority of these come from works that were composed within the three decades following the appearance of the Second Symphony and cloud Mahler's fundamentally diatonic idiom with increasingly ambiguous harmonic propositions. They are also predominantly drawn from composers who were, like Mahler, virtuoso orchestrators: Debussy, Ravel, Strauss, Stravinsky and others. Thus on one level this movement constitutes Berio's *hommage* to past masters of an art that he had himself so assiduously cultivated in the 1950s. There are backward looks to Berlioz – Mahler's great precursor in the art of orchestration – and to the Germanic tradition of

[19] Mahler himself uses this device here and there, so that at FF8 Berio is merely expanding upon his example.

Brahms, Beethoven and Bach, as well as forward to Webern and the Darmstadt school.

The constant fluctuations in harmonic density that result from using this range of reference do not obey any underlying large-scale process of the sort that the vacillating but progressive obliteration of the Mahler produces. Instead, the distribution of these materials is primarily determined by local details within the Mahler text – and later, once that text has begun to disappear, by inter-relations between the quotations themselves. However, a series of groupings by genre is discernible as the movement progresses:

(i) The first is a group of solos from violin concertos, starting at **A19** with the Hindemith *Kammermusik Nr.4* and following this at **C10** with solos from the Berg and Brahms concertos.

(ii) A series of quotations from symphonic scherzos is anticipated at **C2** (the point where Mahler's scherzo itself begins to quote the scherzo of Bruckner's Fourth Symphony) with a quote from Berlioz's *Symphonie fantastique*. A while later, at **E26**, Berio extracts from Ravel's *La Valse* a quotation – conscious or otherwise – from the scherzo of Beethoven's Ninth Symphony, which is immediately followed by a further quote from the Berlioz and one from the scherzo of Mahler's Ninth Symphony.

(iii) Throughout this section there is also a wider dominance of ballet scores, starting with Ravel's *La Valse* (from **D10**) and *Daphnis et Chloé* (**D22**), and progressing, after a return to *La Valse* at **D17** to the 'Danse de la terre' from Stravinsky's *La Sacre du printemps* (from **H15** onwards) and *Agon* (**I6** and **L8**). *La Valse* then returns (**N13** onwards) as ballet gives way to opera.

(iv) The opera in question is *Der Rosenkavalier*, mingled with fragments of *La Valse* after **O**, and returning at **P8**. This is followed after a quiet interval by *Wozzeck* at **S**.

(iv) Finally, the Darmstadt trinity of Webern, Boulez and Stockhausen are presented in close association from **EE**.

The links that are established between Mahler and the superposed or interpolated fragments – and indeed between the fragments themselves – are almost all founded upon one or more of the following features:

(i) common pitches between counterpointed lines;

(ii) the sharing of a common harmonic basis, although in several instances a melodic line is estranged from its original harmonic context in order to combine plausibly with another whose harmonic basis is preserved;

(iii) common melodic shapes.

Since numerous instances of all three processes will be examined in the detailed commentary below, two examples will suffice to illustrate the various possibilities: the quotations from Hindemith's *Kammermusik* and from Berlioz's *Symphonie fantastique*. The Hindemith excerpt illustrates a frequent problem within this movement – that of marrying heterogeneous styles. The passage in question contains several fleeting tonal allusions, but these are far too brief to allow any common harmonic movement. Berio therefore treats it as a partly independent line which, although it contains melodic shapes in common with the Mahler, normally uses only pitch conjunctions as the means for establishing a relationship.

Examples of both occur when the solo line from the Hindemith is first introduced at **A11**. The initial fragment contains shapes that also occur at the beginning and end of the Mahler phrase, whereas the text at **A13** relies upon the common f and $a\flat$ to establish a relationship, as does that at **A16** with its common $c\sharp$. All three are shown in example 19a. When the full violin solo emerges at **A19**, it pursues an independent path until the two converge upon a roughly compatible counterpoint just before **B**. Similar principles of partial independence govern the rest of the Hindemith quotations, the Berg quotation at **C10**, and several others.

The idée fixe from Berlioz's *Symphonie fantastique* provides clearer illustration of the other two modes of relationship. It is first introduced at **C** to provide an augmented version, transposed up a fourth, of Mahler's answer to Bruckner: see example 19b. But when

Ex. 19

it returns at **E12** it instead provides a compatible counterpoint to Trio I, albeit at the cost of its own harmonic identity, as in example 19c. (An even more striking example of original harmonic identity negated occurs when the trumpet solo from *La Valse* is set against that of the Mahler at **P**.)

Similar principles are used to link together chains of quotations once the Mahler text has gone into temporary eclipse. Two of the more striking instances are the use of common upbeat patterns to consummate the garish union of *La Valse* and *Der Rosenkavalier* between **N20** and **P14**, and the analogy established between Bach's first Brandenburg Concerto and Schoenberg's Op.16 no.3 from **Q19** to **R22**.

Chromatic clusters

At one extreme of the harmonic continuum exploited in this movement stands chromatic saturation, both partial (as in the use of small clusters and scales) and total. The clusters appear in three different sections. They are used from the start until just after **D** to 'muddy' the tonal clarity of the Mahler but never to obliterate the outlines, even when the texture becomes comparatively thick, as at **C**. Then they are left in abeyance until Trio II, where they come into their own, entirely obliterating each of the major tonal shifts (from *c* to *d* and from *d* to *e*) that characterize that section. From **N** on, they once again disappear, save for a brief moment during the second reprise, when another cluster formation crowns the quotation from *Wozzeck* at **T**. But, appropriately, when the Trio II materials are recapitulated at **Y** the cluster that first appeared at **K** returns. Other chords – usually not saturated clusters – are used as rapid punctuating agents from the beginning to **B**, at **R**, and in the Boulez quote at **EE**. In the main autonomous events, ungoverned by any englobing process, these will be discussed here only when they contribute to the processes governing the sustained 'blocks'.

A summary of these materials appears in example 20 where black note-heads indicate punctuating chords. It is a general feature of these chords that while the clusters in the upper registers pursue some sort of sequential logic – albeit often rudimentary – the non-saturated, lower portions of each chord are a good deal more idiosyncratic and only occasionally present themselves as parts of a coherent process.

The initial group of cluster materials derives in part from external sources. Thus the initial attack superimposes two clusters: the lower saturating the gamut of the initial chord from the opening quotation of Schoenberg's Op.16 no.4, and the upper covering the same gamut minus a semitone with the major and minor scales of *c* – the key of the Mahler. The saturated *b–f♯* in the strings is similarly derived from the quoted opening of Mahler's Fourth Symphony, and appropriately subsides as the 'correct' Mahler movement is established in its stead, landing on the filled *c–g* fifth. The next

Ex. 20

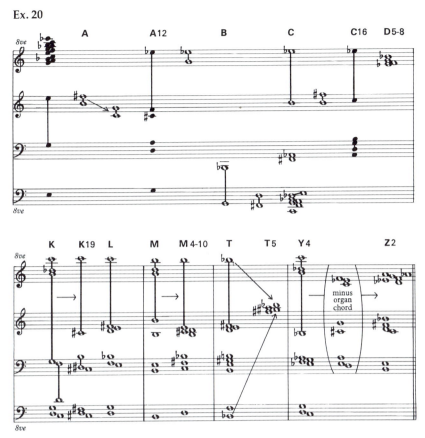

cluster attack reinforces this process by establishing the saturated outlines of the second inversion of the tonic triad. The attack itself also transposes the upper opening cluster attack down an octave, extends it downwards by a tone, and saturates it – thus establishing the $e\flat$ in the top stave as a fixed upper limit for this opening section.

At **B** the c–$e\flat$ cluster passes from strings to wind, thereby ushering in the other main structural feature of these clusters apart from their gamut. For while within string clusters integration of timbre is not a particularly variable factor, clusters for wind or, as later, full orchestra allow for contrast between the classical integration of disparate timbres at one extreme and the juxtaposition of contrasting timbre layers at the other. This first section limits itself to integrated clusters, within which adjacent pitches are preferentially assigned to instruments of different families – the only exception here being the juxtaposition of clarinets 2 and 3. (The attack clusters at the start and after **A** both allow for slightly less stringent integration, but their sheer brevity makes it less than likely that the ear will distinguish the difference.) Inevitably, certain limitations upon integrated timbre-texture may be imposed by the ranges of the instruments themselves, so that the answering cluster that establishes itself in the extreme bass has to use a layer of low brass.

At **C** the upper cluster extends downwards to *b*, while the lower diversifies into the more widespread chordal writing that is to be generally characteristic of the lower register from now on. The *b* in turn briefly reinstates the *b–f♯* cluster from the opening (used here as a sort of harmonic interpretation of the solo cadenza from the Berg Violin Concerto that follows). The full orchestral cluster returns briefly at **C16**, contracting its gamut by a semitone and offering a different but equally integrated orchestration. As the Mahler moves briefly towards *e♭* major after **D**, a non-saturated *e♭–b♭* cluster is produced by flutes and trumpets, fulfilling the same function as its predecessors; but thereafter the device remains in abeyance until its full flowering in Trio II.

Whereas all the examples so far considered have simply been contributions to a multifarious texture, the massive blocks introduced from **K** onwards obliterate all else – and consequently have to sustain musical interest from their own internal resources. The first cluster, at **K**, establishes *c* as a fixed upper limit, and a massive saturated gamut, broken only by two leaps of a tone. The colonising of such high registers necessitates the use of a layer of high violins immediately below the piccolo, but otherwise the texture is rigorously integrated. This time, however, the integration is emphasised, and aurally explored, by assigning to each of five timbre groupings (flutes plus clarinets; 'oboes'[20] and trumpets; horns; 'bassoons' and trombones; strings) differing dynamic curves so that each constantly eclipses the other (a device that had already been thoroughly explored in *Epifanie E*).[21] The voices all start to oscillate around their point of departure; and when they regain stability at **K19**, not only have the tone gaps shifted position – the *d♭–b* gap having descended two octaves – but flute, string, and oboe layers, plus an extensive layer of strings mixed with clarinets, have begun to emerge. When the cluster is reiterated two bars later, at **L**, the transformation is complete. Not only has the gamut of the cluster retracted, but its upper voices are now systematically organised into timbre layers: flutes; clarinets; oboes; strings; trumpets and strings, etc.

Much the same layering pattern is maintained when the next large-scale cluster is unleashed at **M**, quickly growing from its initially restricted formation, emphasising the *b* dominant of Mahler's more or less annihilated *e* major, to a reasonably faithful semitone-downward transposition of the cluster at **L**, varied only in its lower reaches.

The brief re-emergence of another cluster at **T**, capping the proliferating chromatics of the Berg quotation, shifts the upper note down a further semitone, and slightly contracts the cluster's gamut. But while maintaining the layering principle it shuffles the order,

---

[20] Quotation marks here denote a whole timbre grouping – in this case oboes, cor anglais and alto saxophone.

[21] Though the suggestion in Hicks 1981–2 that these are 'quotations' from that piece is incorrect.

which now sounds from the top as: flutes; violins; clarinets; trumpets; 'oboes', etc.

Y recapitulates the cluster at **K**, although slightly modifying the arrangement of pitches below middle *c*. It resolves at **Z2** onto a twelve-note chord whose upper nine pitches progressively contract the intervals between them from major thirds to semitones – scored first for full orchestra, and then for wind and strings in dynamic opposition.

Semantic associations of Mahler's scherzo

So far, commentary has been discussed as a purely formal device in the tradition of the *Chemins*. But with vocal materials and quotations from theatrical or programmatic works all superposed upon a musical 'text' that itself has a wealth of connotations attached to it, Berio is able to accomplish a parallel semantic proliferation and, as a result, to bring this movement closer than any other that he has written to the labyrinthine 'stratification' of Joyce's *Finnegans Wake*. Since Mahler's scherzo was originally associated with a song-text, and he subsequently provided two partly discrepant programmatic descriptions for it, the range of images that may be brought into play is considerable. It is therefore worth separating the various strands:

Song text

(i) *Imagery:* the primary image that Berio borrows from the story of St Anthony preaching to the fishes is that of water, which unites his frequent quotations from Debussy's *La Mer* with a series of fragments that occur between **R** and **Y**. These are: Schoenberg's Op.16 no.3 which, though entitled 'Farben', was described by the composer as being inspired by a lake at dawn (**R11**); the drowning scene from Berg's *Wozzeck* (**S**); the second Water section from Berio's own first movement (**U**); and the 'Scene by the Brook' from Beethoven's Sixth Symphony (**X**). The underlying presence of this image here as in the first and last movements is an essential unifying feature of the work as a whole.

(ii) *Allegory:* Mahler's 'satire upon mankind' centres upon the proposition that although art may move and uplift its audience it will not change the way they behave. A more contemporary view of this theme is introduced by Berio towards the end of the movement, at **AA**. Up to this point, the first tenor has delivered monologues from Beckett's *The Unnamable* (discussed below, p.55). But as the climax gathers force, Berio breaks free of this text to expand upon a quotation from his own article 'Meditation on a Twelve-tone Horse' (Berio 1968) written in the same year as *Sinfonia* – 'all this can't stop the wars, can't make the young older or lower the price of bread',[22] etc. – ending with an absurdly fragile declaration of faith in art,

---

[22] Itself in turn an echo of Brecht's *Das Badener Lehrstück*; see Berio 1985, p.167.

instantly countered by Beckett's 'there must be something else. Otherwise it would be quite hopeless. But it is quite hopeless', etc.

Programmes

At different times, Mahler proposed two partly related images to convey the emotional import of his scherzo. The first was conserved by Natalie Bauer-Lechner after a conversation with Mahler. She records his words as follows:[23]

> If, at a distance, you watch a dance through a window, without being able to hear the music, then the turning and twisting movement of the couples seems senseless, because you are not catching the rhythm that is the key to it all. You must imagine that to one who has lost his identity and his happiness the world looks like this – distorted and crazy, as if reflected in a concave mirror. The Scherzo ends with the appalling shriek of this tortured soul.

The image of the meaningless, maniacal dance seems to have stimulated musical associations for Mahler himself, since the song from *Dichterliebe*, 'Das ist ein Flöten und Geigen', whose final bars end the movement, is itself an alienated description of a wedding ball observed by the bride's abandoned lover.[24] Berio enlarges upon this image, introducing quotations from the second movement ('Le Bal') of Berlioz's *Symphonie fantastique*, whose programme describes a parallel situation, and from Ravel's *La Valse*, whose Viennese lyricism grows increasingly hysterical as the work progresses.

The second, rather more generic image that Mahler suggested for this movement was formulated in a programme for the whole work that Mahler sketched in Berlin in 1901. The first three movements are all described as retrospects upon the life of a dead hero. After the struggles of the first movement, and the temporary idyll of the second, in the third 'the spirit of unbelief, of presumption has taken possession of him, he beholds the tumult of appearances, and together with the child's pure understanding he loses the firm footing that love alone affords; he despairs of himself and of God. The world and life become for him a disorderly apparition; disgust for all being and becoming lays hold of him with an iron grip and drives him to cry out in desperation'.[25] Apart from the evident correlation between this programme and Berio's version of the climax discussed above, this text evokes no musical illustration. Instead, Berio chooses a remarkably apt literary parallel in the form of Beckett's *The Unnamable* to provide the verbal materials for the movement. It is to these that we must now turn.

Sources for the text

Beckett's *L'Innommable* was published in 1952, the last volume of a

---

[23] Bauer-Lechner 1980, pp.43–4.
[24] cf. Tibbe 1971, pp.58–9.
[25] Mitchell 1975, p.183.

trilogy whose other two parts were *Molloy* (1950) and *Malone meurt* (1951). Beckett then produced his own translation into English, which appeared in 1958. Berio presumably chose to work with this latter version because he was writing *Sinfonia* for New York and would otherise have had the complex semantic games of the first, third and fifth movements all played out in French.

The trilogy accomplishes a gradual dissolution of traditional narration and character such that by the third book both are under constant threat. Thus *The Unnamable* presents the monologue of a word-spinning narrator placed in a limbo not unreminiscent of Dante's Divine Comedy, and assailed by voices that seemingly attempt to foist upon him some recognizable character – whether that of Mahood, imprisoned up to his neck in an urn outside a restaurant near the shambles, or the near-insensate Worm, who resists all but the most negative characterization. While the narrator attempts to talk himself into extinction, he is continually propelled back to more or less substantive identity by the fragments of personality with which he believes that his torturers tempt him.[26]

By adopting this text, Berio is able to invert the 'héros tué' theme of the first and second movements. Hero becomes anti-hero. Death deplored becomes death desired. Although within *The Unnamable* there are initially areas of concentration upon the personas of Mahood and Worm, the constantly self-renewing and self-confounding monologue eschews large-scale narrative structure with such determination as to make any résumé by salient fragments, in the manner of the first movement, meaningless.[27] Accordingly, Berio lifts from the text any fragments that suit his purpose. While some of these are simply striking, autonomous images, others are used to comment upon processes at work within the movement and upon the situation within the concert hall itself. Both of these devices will be examined below.

Although Beckett provides the substantial majority of the text, other materials proliferate from it. As well as passing references to Joyce's *Ulysses* and a quotation from Valéry, Berio incorporates titles and written indications from various of the scores involved, solfège, student slogans from the disturbances of the previous spring in Paris, plus the self-quotation noted on p.53. The full range of Berio's vocal resources is employed to articulate these materials – though most of the texts are spoken, leaving solfège or phonemes for the sung sections. Berio also seizes the opportunity to elaborate a multi-voiced version of the flux of dramatic mood already explored in *Sequenza III* for voice. He therefore follows the same method as in

---

[26] For further discussion of this text, and its relation to some of the musical materials, see Hicks 1981–2.

[27] Save that materials from the first Mahood episode, where he spirals inward towards a tower containing his family, are consistently avoided; and that the final and initial materials from the second Mahood episode that shows him imprisoned in an urn are grouped together, between **X** and **Y**.

the previous work, placing different adjectives over the various vocal fragments.[28]

Interactions between text and music

Although most of the interplay between words and music concerns matters of detail, certain features are used to underline the partly submerged contours of Mahler's scherzo. Thus, as the Mahler establishes itself after **A**, materials from the opening sentences of Beckett's text are heard, of which the phrases 'where now?', 'when now?' and particularly 'keep going' are subsequently used to herald each reprise of the scherzo. 'Keep going' also marks the start of Trio I, and the fact that a structural milestone has been reached is further emphasised by the slightly modified Beckett extract that follows: 'Yes, I feel the moment has come for us to look back, if we can, and take our bearings, if we are to go on'. This passage also initiates a large-scale association between the Mahlerian trios and the use of a solo speaker – a device that is amplified on the semantic level by mirroring Beckett's discourse on 'the show' from p.99 of *The Unnamable*, first hinted at in fragments during Trio I (**F3–G10**), but explored at length during Trio II (**L5–R19**), with Berio's own reflections upon 'the show' during the trio reprise (**AA2–CC16**).

The sheer multiplicity of local interactions between text and music is such that proper justice can be done to them only in an inventory set out as below. But they can be categorized initially according to which of the three areas of commentary discussed above they reflect:

(i) The progressive blocking out of the Mahler scherzo. Thus when, at **V6**, the reprise of Trio I is pared down to a static, obsessively reiterated texture, it is prefaced by Beckett's 'I am here so little'. And Berio's final surgery upon Mahler's score, omitting ten bars at **BB5**, follows immediately upon the remark 'for the unexpected is always upon us'.

(ii) Quoted materials: the most richly exploited category. While some of the references are wittily direct – the moment where Stravinsky's 'Danse de la terre' from *Le Sacre du printemps* suddenly gives way to *Agon* is coupled with Beckett's 'the earth would have to quake, it isn't earth' (**I5**), and the reprise at **AA** of some of Berio's earlier quotations from Debussy's *La mer* provokes 'La mer, la mer, toujours recommencée' from Valéry's *Le cimetière marin* – others display a Joycean taste for the recondite. Thus Hindemith's *Kammermusik Nr.4*, dismissed with some scorn after **C**, is ushered in at **A15** with the apparently innocuous 'nothing more restful than chamber music'. Only upon consulting Beckett's text do we discover that the original, at p.105, reads 'nothing more restful than arithmetic'. Again, there is hidden irony behind the rewritten Beckett used to

---

[28] This counterpointing of dramatic mood is a device of long standing in Berio's work, first appearing in *Visage* (1961) and *Passaggio* (1962). It is further developed in *A-Ronne* (1974).

accompany the 'Scene by the Brook' from Beethoven's Sixth Symphony at **X**, 'he shall never hear again hear the lowing cattle, the rush of the stream', since in the original (p.62) this passage described not pastoral bliss but the shambles. It will be recalled that such deflections of a text's original meaning by placing it in a new context were also characteristic of certain portions of the first movement (see pp.14ff).

(iii) Berio's own superposed materials. Some comments are straightforward, such as the first alto's complaint about the insistently repeated high *g* at **C**, or the remarks upon increasingly insistent chromatic scales at **E**. But again there are other more recondite references. When, in the immediately preceding passage at **D**25, the first tenor throws in the phrase 'counting the seconds', keyboards and strings immediately begin to echo each other, as do the two flutes recapitulating the *g* ostinato. Consulting p.78 of Beckett's text, one discovers that the passage from which these three words are taken proposes that, unlike Beckett's Worm, a man would sound out the limits of his confines by crying out and waiting for the echo to return.

An inventory of interrelations

Although the prospect may be a daunting one to any but the more determined reader, the interaction of all the different processes discussed above can be accounted for properly only in a bar-by-bar study of Berio's score. Granted the exuberant variety of relations that proliferate throughout the movement, both intra-musical and between music and text, it would be foolish to claim that the survey which follows is in any way exhaustive. But it does nonetheless seek to record all significant interactions between materials from different sources, though indicating only in outline those large-scale processes that have already been discussed.

Rehearsal letters have been used to divide the account, with bar numbers counted from each letter as in the rest of this text. All references to the Mahler scherzo are given as Ma. followed by the bar number. All references to other scores follow the sequence: composer, title, movement (if the work is so divided), rehearsal number (in italics), bar number (counted from the previous rehearsal number when these are present, or otherwise from the beginning). All references to Beckett's *The Unnamable* are to the Calder & Boyars edition of 1975, and are given as Beck. followed by the page number. All orchestral instruments are referred to by the Italian abbreviations found in the score, with Str standing for strings, and WW for woodwind.

1 Tr & Tbn: Schoenberg, *Fünf Orchesterstücke*, Op.16 no.4 ('Peripetie'), 2; Str, then WW & Cor play the accompanying string chord.
2 (i) Voices take over the brass chord, announcing the title of the Schoenberg; Vni B, Vc & Cb take over the accompanying chord.

(ii) Fl 1 & 2, Grelots: Mahler, Fourth Symphony, 1st movement, 1, while Vni C chromatically fill its bare fifth.

(iii) Vni A: Debussy, *La Mer*, III, 54 5 (cf. the accompanying *db* triad, inexplicitly present in T, B & Cb 2 of Berio's accompaniment). This is the first water reference in the movement and the source of a number of subsequent quotations.

4 (i) WW, Vni B, Vc, Cb & Harp: Debussy, *La Mer*, II, 1. The bare fifth and flattened sixth transpose those of the Mahler Fourth Symphony opening up a tone, thus establishing positions on either side of the goal: the *c, g* and *ab* of the opening of Mahler's scherzo.

(ii) T 1: direction from the score of Mahler's Fourth Symphony.

5 S 1 announces title of Debussy.

6 (i) Vni B: Mahler, Fourth Symphony, 3. A filled fourth anticipates the *g–c* of the next few bars.

(ii) B 1 announces the accompanying direction in the score.

(iii) Pf develops the harp gesture from Debussy.

7 (i) The Mahler scherzo finally enters (cf. Ma.10).

(ii) S 2 and A 2 name both Mahler symphonies.

A

1 Cl 2 acciaccaturas echo those of Mahler's Fourth Symphony.

2 (i) Pf and Harp underline the harmonic relationship between Debussy and Mahler.

(ii) Voices confuse the issue as to which movement is to be played.

3 B 1 announces the direction at Ma.1.

5 S & A begin solfège analysis of fragments of Mahler melody – a device that frequently recurs.

8 (i) Sxf a: a warped anticipation of Ma.19.

(ii) B 1: Beck.7.

10 T 2: Beck.7.

11 (i) Fl & Ott: Schoenberg, Op.16 no.4, 3, down one tone (though this figure appears elsewhere at pitch in the Schoenberg without the piccolo note).

(ii) Vni B: Hindemith, *Kammermusik Nr.4 (Violinkonzert)*, Op.36, no.3, 5th movement, 1. To be used extensively. Although its opening three notes transpose Mahler's opening, here it is the *g–f♯–g/d–c♯–d* relationship that is emphasised.

13 Sxf a: Hindemith, *op. cit.*, 2: *f* and *ab* in common with Ma.

15 T 2: Beck.105 rewritten with reference to Hindemith. Original: 'Nothing more restful than arithmetic'.

16 Hindemith, *op. cit.*, 3.

18 (i) S 2 comments on Mahler's scoring.

(ii) B 1: Beck.7.

19 Vn solo: Hindemith starts again in its true medium.

20 Fl 1 & Ob 1: Debussy, *La Mer*, III, 54 7. Accompanying Vn harmonic starts to thicken into a cluster just as its identity is affirmed.

22 Berio begins to rescore individual instrumental lines of the Mahler in a more fragmented fashion (cf. Ma.31). Thus Mahler's Vn 2 line is passed from Sxf a, Sxf t and A 1, the re-entering melody in the next bar is divided among Str and S, etc.

B

1 (i) The *g–e♭* gamut of Mahler's fragmented Vn 2 line is now transposed and saturated to form a WW cluster that clouds both the initial *c* minor and the ensuing *e♭* major.

(ii) Vn solo: Hindemith, *op. cit.*, **L4**.

2 Tbn 1 starts an analogous bass cluster.

3 Vn solo leaps to Hindemith, *op. cit.*, **P8**.

5 (i) Mahler by now entirely transferred to vocal solfège plus pizz. lower strings.

(ii) Vn solo: Hindemith, *op. cit.*, **Q4**.

10 Tr continue motion of Hindemith on monotone *g*.

C

1 (i) Cemb carries on momentum of Hindemith, soon joined by Pf (its see-saw motion not unreminiscent of Hindemith from *op. cit.*, **O** onward).

(ii) High cluster extends downwards (see ex.20).

(iii) Fl & Ob 1: adapted from Berlioz, *Symphonie fantastique*, 2nd movement, 120, imitating the Mahler at **C2** in augmentation.

2 T 1 & B 2 dismiss the Hindemith.

4 (i) S 2: Beck.11.

(ii) A 1 reacts to ostinato *g*.

6 T 1: clearly a Joycean reference, though its source has not yet been traced.

8 (i) S 1: Beck.14.

(ii) Vni C re-establish the *b–f♯* cluster: cf. opening bars.

9 (i) A 1: Beck.11.

(ii) B 1: Beck.12.

10 (i) T 1: origin unknown.

(ii) Vn solo: Berg, Violin Concerto, 2nd movement, 5, sharing common *b* and *b♭* with Mahler (Cl).

13 (i) B 1: transforms the Beckett quote of **C9** into a comment on the Vn solo.

(ii) Vn solo jumps to Berg, *op. cit.*, 1st movement, 169, while amplifying Mahler's move towards a minor climax.

14 (i) Vni B develop Mahler into tremolo.

(ii) T 1: Beck.78.

15 Voices solfège Berg.

16 (i) Vn solo switches to an equally rhapsodic gesture from Brahms, Violin Concerto, 2nd movement, 48.

17 A 2 underlines this transition.

20 Fg & Cfg elaborate upon Ravel, *La Valse*, 26 4–6, the first of many quotes from this work. It is identical with the third bar of the main Mahler theme (cf. **D3**, Vni A), and recurs frequently during the next few pages.

22 T 1 identifies the Ravel, subtitled a 'Poème chorégraphique', but runs on into Beck.73 to create an apparent description of the 'poème' out of a passage that originally alluded to the 'torturers'.

D

4 (i) Fl 2 tremolo begins a new cluster.

(ii) Vni C begin a triplet heterophony around Mahler.

5 Mahler is subjected to a variety of further heterophonic distortions:
   (i) Ob & Cl reduce it to a skeleton of repeated notes.
   (ii) Vni B play one semiquaver late.
   (iii) Vle add glissandi.
9 Vni propose a new distortion of Mahler through continuous jumps in octave transposition.
10 Brass: the ♪♫ rhythm first introduced in the Mahler at the previous bar (in WW) instantly provokes an emphatic interruption in the same rhythm from brass and percussion. Although this gesture derives from Ravel, *op. cit.*, 36–9 and 63–6, and will appear as such at E23, its harmony here is derived from the omnipresent bass figure first heard at C20. Snare drum continues the rhythm as an ostinato.
12 (i) Fl: Ravel, *op. cit.*, 32. This quote continues in Fl & Vni through to D21, though truncated by one bar. The chromatic accompaniment rapidly expands into an autonomous WW & keyboard 'cloud' (cf. Stravinsky, *Le Sacre du printemps*, 34–7, for a precursor of such textures). This is the first of several elaborations upon chromatic materials.
   (ii) T 1: Beck.12.
15 A 1 rephrases Beckett in ironic reference to chromatic proliferation.
22 Fl 1: Ravel, *Daphnis et Chloé*, 176 4, down a semitone.
23 T 1 identifies the flute quote but, whether through misprint or design, alters Daphnis's sex. According to Altmann 1977, p.32, the curious description 'written in red' refers not to some dandyish predilection for multi-coloured scores on Ravel's part but to the cover of an RCA recording of the work.
24 Staccato wind chord based on scales of *c* minor underlines Ravel quote.
25 T 1: Beck.78. In the original this refers to the possibility of exploring one's confines by listening for echoes – a means of resolving the problem alluded to by T 1 at C14. It immediately unleashes echo effects on flutes, keyboards and strings.
27 Fl 2 & Ott take up the obsessional *g* from *Daphnis*.
30 A 1 underlines the chromatic element in the Mahler.

E

1 Cl 1 declares chromatic independence, and ends chasing the Vn solo at E3.
2 Ob & Vn solo: Debussy, *La Mer*, II ('Jeux de vagues'), 24 2: a further exploration of the chromatic, as S 2 notes.
3 T 1: Beck.104, used to comment on the formal situation as Mahler dissolves into one portion of the 'Jeux de vagues', which then dissolves into another. Berio acknowledges this latter by rewriting the end of the quotation.
4 Vni & Vle join the Debussy.
6 (i) C i joins the Debussy.
   (ii) Having reached Trio I (Ma.103), Mahler's text goes underground, asserting its existence only by occasional fragments.
7 (i) WW & Vc continue Debussy, while Vn solo, which should by now be silent, fixates on the last eight notes of its solo.
   (ii) S 1 misquotes Mahler.
9 (i) Debussy, *op. cit.*, 19.
   (ii) B 1 misquotes Mahler.
11 (i) Cl 1 & Ob 1 extend and develop Debussy motif.

(ii) A 1 takes *b* from Debussy WW to revert to Mahler.

(iii) B 2: Beck.52.

(iv) Debussy cello figure leads back into:

12 (i) A similar figure from Mahler.

(ii) Fl 1, Ob 1, Vni A & B & Vle: Berlioz, *Symphonie fantastique*, 2nd movement, 122.

16 (i) Vni C: harmonic from Debussy, *op. cit.*, 54 5, returns.

(ii) End of Berlioz provokes:

17 (i) Ob 2, Fg 1 & Str: Ravel, *La Valse*, 18 7.

(ii) Sn drum directs attention back to ♩.♪♪ rhythm, in preparation for E23.

18 Further chromatic interference from keyboards.

19 T 1: Beck.52.

23 Fl, Ob, Fg & Tr: Ravel, *op. cit.*, 38 10, takes over from keyboard chromatics, leading into Ravel's own quotation, involuntary or otherwise, of the scherzo from Beethoven's Ninth Symphony at E26. The Beckett quotation in T 1 reflects both this and the recurrent 'obsession with the chromatic' that pervades this section.

F

1 T 1: Beck.97.

4 (i) Mahler in Vni B is compared with Berlioz, *Symphonie fantastique*, 2nd movement, 154 (Vni C).

(ii) T 1: Beck.99 rewritten in 1960s jargon. We are to return to this discourse on 'the show' at length in Trio II.

(iii) Fl 2: chromatic end of Ravel and Mahler converge upon:

5 Fl & Cl: Berlioz, *op. cit.*, 156, rewritten to accompany the other Berlioz quote in Vni C. It leads into:

8 (i) orchestra: Mahler, Ninth Symphony, 2nd movement, *20*, thus echoing the previous 'Ninth Symphony' interruption at E26.

(ii) B 1: Unknown source, but clearly provoked by Mahler's Ninth.

9 (i) Fl only sustain a rewritten version of Mahler's Ninth Symphony altered to fit:

(ii) Str & Cor, which revert to the Mahler 'text'.

G

4 Tr: rhythm similar to several wind figures from Debussy's 'Jeux de vagues', but identical with none.

5 B 1: Beck.99.

6 Harp establishes a *c/f* ♯ polarity, with fifths in organum, immediately taken up by the Tr. This polarity is to become a pivotal feature uniting Stravinsky's 'Danse de la terre' at H15 and Debussy's 'Dialogue du vent et de la mer' at J.

9 Fl & Vni: a minor mystery. None of the commentaries on this movement can suggest a source for this interpolation, nor can Berio recall it. A source for the rhythmic combination might be the 2nd movement of Mahler's Second Symphony (cf. for instance b.68), which Berio had at one point planned to use as the basis for this movement. But there are no corresponding pitch sequences.

11 Fragments of Mahler have been heard with greater insistence over the previous pages. Here, with the first reprise, it takes over completely.

24 B 1: Beck.22, a possible reference to the incursion, as from the next bar, of Berio's favoured device of heterophonic elaboration.

H

1 (i) Vni A & B alternate with keyboards in delaying and 'flurrying' Mahler's Vn parts.

(ii) The texture is further thickened by voices being required to imitate given instrumental lines.

(iii) Sxf start a final process of chromatic proliferation, reflecting Mahler's own usage from **H5**.

2 T 1: Beck.99.

5 Vc join the chromatic quagmire.

11 Quickening chromatic motion prepares:

15 Stravinsky, *Le Sacre du printemps*, 'Danse de la terre', *75* 11. This starts in Timp and Vni B & C, but spreads immediately to the whole orchestra save keyboards, who continue almost unheard with the two violin parts from the Mahler. However, the version of the Stravinsky that ensues is more bizzarely distorted than any previous manipulations to which Mahler has been subjected. **H**16–23 are eight bars, whereas the corresponding Stravinsky *76* to *77* are nine; but each stratum of the texture omits a bar at a different place. Thus Vni, Vle & Vc amalgamate b.2 & b.3 of the extract; the Timp part compresses b.3–5 into two bars of *c*/*f*♯ oscillation; WW and Cb omit b.6; Cor omit b.8; and Tr, omitting nothing, are left one bar out at the end. The harp mediates between discrepant Vc and Cb parts.

24 Str & WW: one bar's reversion to Mahler.

25 Stravinsky, *op. cit.*, *77* 5.

26 Back to Mahler.

27 Back to Stravinsky, *78*.

I

2 (i) Fl: encapsulation of Mahler.

(ii) T 1: Beck.81, underlining the earth theme just before the 'Danse de la terre' disappears.

4 Stravinsky, *op. cit.*, final bar of 'Danse de la terre'.

5 (i) answered by brass chord from Mahler leading into Trio II.

(ii) Timp contrasts *c*/*f*♯ polarity of Stravinsky with the *c*/*g* of Mahler.

6 Str: Stravinsky, *Agon*, 'Double Pas-de-Quatre', 61.

7 (i) T 1 uses Beckett quote to underline passage from 'Danse de la terre' to *Agon*.

(ii) The three Vc and Cb upbeats to Trio II lead to nothing save high flute *c*s.

(iii) Timp match this with the low *c* from Debussy, *La Mer*, III, 1.

8 The start of Trio II (Ma.190), like that of Trio I, submerges into fragments. These are in constant interaction with two other protagonists: Stravinsky's *Agon*, and Debussy's 'Dialogue du vent et de la mer' from *La Mer*.

(i) Ob, Fg & upper Str: Stravinsky, 61.

(ii) Vc & Cb: Mahler contrasted with:

9 Debussy, 2.

10 (i) Mahler.

(ii) A 1: Beck.35.

(iii) T 1 describes 'Double Pas-de-Quatre'.

11 Debussy, 4.

12 Ob, Fg & Str: Stravinsky, 62.

13 Lower Str: Debussy, 6.

J

1 (i) Cl, Ob, Tr, Timp (cf. **H**15) & Cb: Debussy, *43* 1.
   (ii) Other Str: Stravinsky, 73.
   (iii) A 1: source unknown.
   (iv): T 1: Beck.101.
2 Low Str: Mahler.
3 Stravinsky, 76.
5 Low Str: Mahler, using common *g* from Stravinsky.
6 & 7 (i) C 1, Fg, low Str: Debussy, *43* 6.
      (ii) T 1 repeats Beck.22.
7 Str (save Vni C): Mahler.
8 T 1: Beck.52, this time presumably referring to his repetition of Beck.22.
9 (i) Castagn: Stravinsky, *Agon*, 'Bransle Gay', 310.
   (ii)Str (save Vni C): Stravinsky, *op. cit.*, 'Triple Pas-de-Quatre', 102, an approximate transposition of the Mahler, to which they instantly revert.
10 (i) Fl 3 & Ott resume high *c* of the opening to Trio II in response to the Debussy *c* from low WW.
   (ii) Fl & Vni C: Stravinsky, *Agon*, 108, which rapidly spreads to the whole ensemble.
14 Brass upbeat to first large tonal step in the Mahler (to *d* major) encounters:

K

1 (i) massive cluster (see ex. 20 on p.51) that separates into four agglomerates, each with its own intensity pattern.
   (ii) The only detail to break through is the independent timp line, in part a continuation of Stravinsky's 'Bransle Gay' rhythm.
5 Str: Mahler fragment.
7 Cor: Mahler fragment.
11 All parts start independent semitonal shifts around their original note. Aggregate rhythms increase to repeated semiquavers. Dynamic contrasts reduce to WW vs. Str.
19 The new aggregate thus established displaces the 'break' in the cluster ($d\flat/b$) by two octaves, and shifts bass notes by semitones. By now, dynamics are unified.
20 Repeat of the brass upbeat to this section (not present in the Mahler original).

L

1 Another huge cluster, this time with layered scoring.
2 Vc initiate a return to the Mahler,
4 (i) which, however, is radically reorchestrated: Vn 2 becomes Fl; Ob becomes A 1; low Str becomes Bongos.
   (ii) Ott, Ob & Org add high drone, harmonically complementing Mahler.
   (iii) Castagn revert to Stravinsky's 'Bransle Gay'.
5 (i) Str (plus Timp) interrupt periodically with their layer of the cluster from **L**1.
   (ii) T 1 begins a long narration from Beck.99 on the nature of the entertainment in hand. This provides some measure of unity as the Mahler becomes increasingly fragmented or obliterated.
8 Another passage closely integrating materials from *Agon*, 'Triple Pas-de-Quatre', and fragments of Mahler:

(i) Tr & Vle: Stravinsky, 106, combined by both pitch and phrase-shape with:

(ii) B 2: slightly warped version of Mahler.

9 (i) Tr make a unified phrase out of Stravinsky and Mahler.

(ii) Tbn: Stravinsky, *loc. cit.*

10 (i) Fg 1 & Vni A take over Stravinsky.

(ii) Fl & B take on Mahler's Vn and Vc parts.

11 (i) Fl & Tr: Stravinsky, 107.

(ii) A 1 takes on Mahler's Cl part.

(iii) Vni B link Mahler with:

12 Stravinsky, *loc. cit.*

13 (i) Tbn & Tuba imitate their previous Stravinsky material in order to underline a Mahlerian progression.

(ii) Cl: Mahler.

14 (i) Fl & Vni: Stravinsky, 108.

(ii) Tr, Pf & Vc: Mahler.

15 Pf, Cemb & Cb continue Mahler, distorted by irregular octave doublings from the two keyboards.

17 Tr combines the two upper lines of the Mahler, as does Fl in the next bar.

18 Cb pizz. *d* acts as catalyst for return of Stravinsky, 61.

20 Tr & Ott continue their previous gesture with an independent scale.

22 Ob, Fg & Str recapitulate Stravinsky, 61.

23 Cl: Mahler.

25 Mahlerian upbeat again leads to:

M

1 (cf. Ma.257) a more layered cluster, the gamut of whose upper group contracts by a semitone at either extremity the analogous group in the cluster at **K** (see ex.20). This quickly fills out into a fuller cluster whose upper components (down to the g of Tr 1) transpose the analogous components of the cluster at **L** down a semitone. Strings momentarily penetrate with the Mahler.

3 Sxf t, Fg & low Str: a further Mahler fragment.

5 Layered dynamics are again used.

12 (i) Fl: Mahler's Vn part (cf. Ma.268) modified by leaping to positions within:

(ii) a series of less dense wind aggregates using the rhythm of Ma.269.

13 Strings resume their chromatic shifting.

15 (i) Timp plays Mahler figure that should have occurred four bars previously. This and the misplaced rhythm of **M12** are the first hints of the major metric dislocations to come.

N

1 Mahler returns in the Tr quartet and Harp, with Pf and Cemb playing 2nd Harp, and Sxf supplying Vn part until Str take over. Str, however, descend slowly from the registers established by their **M15** cluster, providing a lush, widely spaced background that adds a patina of Straussian indulgence to the direct, rather spare nostalgia of the Mahler score. The Vn 2 line is thrown from part to part.

9 S 1 takes Mahler's Vn 1 part.

13 Fl superimposes Ravel, *La Valse, 32.*

17 (i) Fl jumps two bars in the Ravel.
(ii) Contrary motion chromatics (an exaggeration of the missing Ravel accompaniment) in WW and Str blur:
(iii) Mahler, played by remaining wind.
(iv) Tamb displaces 'Bransle Gay' rhythm.

20 The start of an episode exploiting the common upbeat pattern of sections from Ravel's *La Valse* and Act II of Strauss's *Der Rosenkavalier* that almost entirely obliterates the Mahler.
(i) WW & Vc: Ravel, *78* 2.
(ii) Timp combine rhythm of Mahler, low Str, with pitch of Ravel.
(iii) Similarly, Vni C develop Mahler's Vn figuration, at first following Ravel's harmony.

22 A 1 joins Beckett narration.

23 S 1: Mahler fragments, passed to T 1 and back.

25 (i) Cor adapts Ravel's chromaticism to lead into:
(ii) Strauss, *Der Rosenkavalier*, II, *250,* with a touch of parody added through stuttering Cor and glissando Vc. The Cl line adds an upbeat flourish to the end of the previous section.

0

1 Ob counteracts *Rosenkavalier* with Ravel, *81* 6, then jumps a bar as:

2 *Rosenkavalier* dissolves into its counterpart at Ravel, *82.*

6 Another bar of *Rosenkavalier*, II, *254* 10, with a counterpoint inserted by Berio on Tr and middle Str, facilitates the jump to:

7 Ravel, *92* 3.

12 Ott, Fl 1 & Cl picc enter over Ravel with Strauss, *253* 5.

13 The rest of the orchestra join in, but immediately:

14 S 1 enters over Strauss with Mahler.

P

1 (i) Tr 2 & A 1 help re-establish Mahler, while Tr 1, in duet with Tr 2, plays a transposed version of the solo from Ravel, *67* – which thus acquires a new harmonic interpretation, centring on the dominant rather than the submediant.
(ii) Fg 2 & Tuba: source unknown.

5 Fl: Vn 2 transposed (while Vni B instead anticipate next bar), leading to:

6 (i) retrograde of Mahler's scale, carried on into **P**7 by Vni C, and ending on a high $f\sharp$ that is the last relic of the Mahler text before its metric underpinning is lost for the first time.
(ii) A 1 starts a vocal line (proceeding to S 2 & 1) that combines the Marschallin's moment of final renunciation at *293* of *Rosenkavalier*, Act III (up a semitone) with Oktavian's vocal line at *298* 7 – by which time the orchestra is playing the same passage.

7 Vni B & Vle introduce:

8 WW, Cor, Vni C & low Str: Strauss, *op. cit.*, Act III, *298* 5, again with satirical touches. Vni A & B and Vc add passing notes. Vc at **P**10 substitute an outrageous double sharp for Strauss's $f\sharp$. Pf, Harp & Vle render the texture extravagantly lush.

9 Fl & Ott maintain an independent line, taking over the Vni C $f\sharp$ that echoes the missing Tr line of Ma.316.

14 Pf & Str: the final chord from the *Rosenkavalier* quote recalls Ma.317–18.

16 (i) Fl & Vni A encapsulate Ma.318–19, and then join:
(ii) Vni B and Ob 1, which anticipate the Brahms quotation at **Q**.

18 (i) Cfg, Tr & low Str take up Ma.320. Thus, since $\mathbf{P}$ = Ma.309, six bars have been added – the first of a number of distortions of Mahler's metric framework.

(ii) Fl complements previous chromatics by a descent from its high $f\sharp$.

19 T 2 relays instruction from Mahler's score.

Q

1 (i) Fl & upper Str: over the e minor added sixth chord enters Brahms, Fourth Symphony, 4th movement, 69.

(ii) T 1 inserts into the Beckett narration an acknowledgement of the Brahms quote.

3 (i) Vle speed up Brahms's rate of flow, while Fl 1 ornaments it.

(ii) Voices solfège Brahms.

(iii) Pf & Cemb take up their characteristic semiquaver movement, developing the fixed anchoring pitch of the Brahms in a manner reminiscent of the first movement (cf. **K**).

7 Sn drum, followed by Bongos, outline the Cb figure from the Mahler one bar late.

8 Mahler's text begins to be treated with increasing freedom as the music once again cuts free of its metric proportions:

(i) Ott plays an inversion of the main WW material from the Mahler, answered by Ob, entering two bars early and a third higher.

(ii) T 1 quits his Beckett narration to comment on 'crossed colours', referring both to the crossing instrumental lines and to Pousseur's *Couleurs croisées*, of which a stylistic pastiche follows from **Q**14. He then jumps to Beck.103.

(iii) Cb develops Ma.328 too late.

11 Although in the Mahler the Tr choir stops its alternating chords here, Berio continues to reiterate them obsessively, passing them to the oboes in preparation for the Bach quote at **Q**19.

12 Another reference to *Couleurs croisées*, which is based upon transformations of the song 'We shall overcome'.

14 (i) T 1: however, it is not Henri Pousseur, but Beckett who says 'if this noise' etc (Beck.92).

(ii) Harp, Pf & Cemb embark on a pastiche characteristic of the textures and instrumentation of *Couleurs croisées*, though without actual quotation from the score (*pace* Altmann 1977, p.35, where an erroneous reference is given).

16 Ob 1 sharpens the c of the Mahler chord, and Fg 1 enters on an a producing a dominant seventh (plus minor ninth from Fl in the next bar) resolving onto the Bach quote in **Q**19.

17 T 1 resumes his narration from Beck.99.

19 Alternately Fg & low Str, Ob, upper Str: Bach, first Brandenburg Concerto, 2nd movement, last 4 bars, but with $b\natural$ for $b\flat$ in the penultimate bar.

R

5 Bach speeds up from units of four quavers to three quavers.

9 (i) Bach slows down again at cadence.

(ii) Cl 1 picks out e an octave below that on to which Vni B must resolve and:

10 is joined by Fg 2 $g\sharp$, both preparing:

11 (i) Fl, Cl, Fg & Vle: Schoenberg, *Fünf Orchesterstücke*, Op.16 no.3 ('Farben'), 2. As well as reflecting the alternating timbres of the Bach, this quotation also recalls the alternating chords of the missing Mahler text.

(ii) S 1: Beck.109, modified by the addition of 'in a lake full of colours' so as to acknowledge Schoenberg's 'Farben' (colours) which in the 1949 revision had the title 'Sommermorgen an einem See'. The quotation also anticipates the drowning scene from *Wozzeck* that begins at **S**, and constitutes the first link in a chain of water references.

(iii) Vc begin a series of metrically dislocated fragments from Mahler – here Ma.330 with the g sharpened to accord with the Schoenberg.

12 Vni C join in Ma.331.

13 Vc switch back to Ma.330 as Vni C continue with Ma.332.

16 Vni C & Vc: Ma.334 (Vc again sharpen g).

18 Vni C & Vc: Ma.335.

19 Vni B: Ma.339.

20 (i) Fl 3, Vni A & B: Ma.342.

(ii) Cfg prepares a re-establishment of Mahler: cf. Ma.340.

21 (i) Schoenberg jumps one bar to the second half of 5.

(ii) S & A: Ma.343 without accidentals.

(iii) B: Ma.339 in the shape of Ma.333.

22 Vni C: Ma.338.

23 Mahler's text re-established (cf. Ma.342) twenty-two bars late. Tr 1's eb is common to both Schoenberg and Mahler, and the long held low Str c resolves, as in Mahler, onto db.

S

1 The WW's chromatic descent in the previous bar evokes by way of response not the 2nd scherzo reprise, but:

(i) Vc & Cb, plus Vle a bar later: Berg, *Wozzeck*, Act III, 284, the point at which Wozzeck drowns, overheard by the Captain and the Doctor.

(ii) Fg and Guiro maintain the Mahler, which is once again subject to fragmentation and encapsulation.

2 Wind & Vni combine Ma.349 and Ma.351.

3 (i) S 1 carries on Ma.352.

(ii) A 1 comments on Wozzeck's murder of Marie.

(iii) B 1: Wozzeck's last word (though not with the intonation indicated by Berg).

4 (i) WW play Ma.353–5 simultaneously, thus producing a cluster to match the Berg.

(ii) B 2 also comments on Wozzeck.

5 (i) Fl, with interjections from Tr and Vni C, superimpose a slowly ascending major third cluster that is finally to establish itself, at **T10**, as that of the second Water section from the first movement. But for the moment it complements and thickens the texture of the Berg.

(ii) Fg encapsulate Ma.354–7.

(iii) S: Ma.355.

7 (i) A 1 initiates, several bars early, the conversation between the Captain and the Doctor as Wozzeck drowns.

(ii) T 1: Beck.89.

8 (i) Cl 1, joined subsequently by other WW: Ma.361–3.

(ii) B 1 carries on the Captain's initial remark.

10 Cl 1 & low WW start the next chromatic ascent from Berg.
13 The Mahler is temporarily re-established, nine bars early. Thus Ma.369 starts from Vle, adding Vni plus, in S16, Cor 1 playing Cl 1 of the Mahler, and Cfg playing Fg 1 of the Mahler.
16 B 1 switches to the German text of Wozzeck.
17 (i) S takes over Mahler line, with rhythmic distortion from A and Vni A.
(ii) Low Str start the next ascent from *Wozzeck*, but:
18 (i) this turns into a precipitous glissando, abetted by:
(ii) WW, who likewise abandon the Berg, speeding up the tempo of their chromatic scales.
(iii) meanwhile with S & A Mahler is once again lost.
19 B 1 continues the Captain's words in English, while orchestra builds to:

T

1 Another briefly held large cluster whose upper limit shifts downwards by a further semitone (cf. **K** and **M** as well as ex.20).
2 (i) Again, the text of *Wozzeck* in English and German.
(ii) Meanwhile the cluster immediately begins to reduce to:
5 the filled major third from the second Water section of the first movement (at **E**).
10 The polyrhythmic texture of the Water section is restored.

U

3 A: source unknown.
4 Cl: Ma.396; Vni B: retrograde of same.
5 Cb follow on with Ma.397, with which they continue, fixating on the $d\flat$ until the other parts, delayed by two bars of Berio, can join them.
7 Fl 1, Cl 1: Ma.397, upon which Cl picc provides heterophonic elaboration.
8 (i) S take up the oscillation f–e, to be sustained with melancholy persistence during the coming bars.
(ii) Vni begin a slow descent from their $g\flat$–$b\flat$ cluster towards an e–g cluster that heralds the return of the Mahler.
10 Cl 1 mixes Fl 3 & Fl 2 parts of Mahler, harmonized by S oscillation,
12 as does Fl 1.
13 S oscillation generates upbeat to:

V

1 Mahler re-established (cf. Ma.402), this time having gained two bars in the process.
4 (i) T 1: presumably Beckett, but untraced.
(ii) Sn drums adds a second ostinato, projecting the 'Bransle Gay' rhythm into a four-quaver unit.
5 WW joins in the e–f oscillation.
6 This should mark the start of the trio reprise, but Berio now embarks on his most startling Mahlerian transformation yet. Taking as his cue the f drone that pervades much of this section of the original, Berio freezes fragments of Mahler's material into a doggedly persistent ostinato, against which piano and sections of the solo violin part present two sections of the Mahler grossly distorted by octave transposition and, at times, rhythmic encapsulation. While the whole episode up to **Y** lasts 34 bars in both Mahler and Berio, the two portions used (Ma.408–23 and

Ma.434–40) are both displaced from their original positions within this framework.

(i) An ostinato is built from Vc & Timp (Ma.407) plus Org & Cemb (Ma.433).

(ii) Fg continues Mahler's chromatic scale, which ends on U10 with the Cb drone.

(iii) Meanwhile Vni C glissando through two octaves to establish another high cluster on *a–c*.

9 T 1: Beck.81, an appropriate response to four concurrent ostinati.

11 Pf starts its distortion of Ma.408.

W

1 Solo Vn. joins in with an equally distorted version, whose *b* leads into:

2 a return of Hindemith, *Kammermusik Nr.4 (Violinkonzert)*, Op.36 no.3, **P**16. (It will be recalled that this work was previously the cause of some exasperation – which its reappearance amidst this lunar landscape does nothing to diminish).

3 (i) Vn solo: Hindemith restored to its original speed.

(ii) Pf: the pitches of this and the following two bars derive from the WW figure that accompanies the Vn in Hindemith's *Kammermusik*, the rhythm of which, at half speed, coincides with the ostinato into which the 'Bransle Gay' has been transformed.

6 Pf and Vn solo each provide their own version of Ma.414, which the Pf continues.

7 (i) Vn solo resumes Hindemith at the appropriate point.

(ii) The ostinati are progressively subtracted from this point, starting with the *e–f* oscillation.

8 (i) T 1 switches to commentary on Beckett (with echoes of Beck.107).

(ii) Vn solo continues down the scale started on the first beat of the bar so as to lead into:

9 a similarly distorted version of the WW material from Ma.417 (at which the Pf has also arrived).

12 Vn solo takes string line from Pf for one bar.

13 (i) Pf carries on with Ma.421–3.

(ii) Meanwhile Vle start Ma.434, and thereafter Str progressively substantiate the reference, through to Ma.340 (**W**18).

14 (i) Vn solo takes up Hindemith at the point where it had broken off.

(ii) Vc and Timp ostinato ceases.

15 Timp accompany Ma.423 in Pf.

16 Pf suddenly switches to the rival Mahler passage in the Str (Ma.437).

17 Cor, Org & Cemb ostinato ceases, having failed to coordinate with Ma.437 from which it originated.

19 (i) The last of the ostinati – on Sn drum – ceases.

(ii) *e♭* implications of Mahler from Vni B, plus the oscillating solo Vn figures usher in Beethoven, Sixth Symphony, 2nd movement ('Scene by the Brook'), 69.

(iii) To this T 1 responds with an apparently apt Beckett quote, 'he shall never again hear the lowing cattle' (Beck.62) – one of Berio's darker jokes, since what is described in the original is a slaughter house.

X

4 Cor takes over Fg figures from Beethoven and holds it awaiting the return of the Mahler.

6 T 1: Beck.43, with 'more' misprinted for 'move'.

9 T 1 to 'no one': Beck.44. What follows is from an unknown source, but refers to Vinko Globokar's *Voie* on a text by Mayakovsky.

Y

1 The reprise of Trio II is allowed to start unimpaired, but:

3 immediately begins to be submerged under a rapidly growing cluster (see ex. 20 on p.51), beneath which the metric structure once again becomes lost. Vni A derives from Ma.445.

4 The cluster is completed: it recapitulates that heard at **K** with minor variations in the register just below middle *c*.

7 Mahler briefly re-emerges, with upper Str playing Ma.450 and low Str Ma.449. Both unite on Ma.451 in the next bar.

12 The complete cluster is re-established.

Z

2 A shift to a new harmonic basis, fully established by **Z**3. The keyboard punctuations are to survive as a unifying feature until almost the end of the movement, thereby matching the earlier use of ostinati.

8 The same chord is now taken up by Str vs. WW, each following its own dynamic pattern with a gradual accelerando in rates of change.

AA

1 Berio now starts to recapitulate and develop materials used at the start of the movement in a parallel gesture to the missing Mahler:
(i) Opening chord plus Schoenberg, cf. b.1. Whether by printer's error or composer's design, Cor 3 & 4 now play $b\natural$ and $f\natural$ and Vni A $c\sharp$ and a (though the 1969 score has the expected notes from b.1).
(ii) As before, WW substitute for Cb.

2 (i) This is immediately followed by Debussy, *La Mer*, III.
(ii) T 1 now embarks on another monologue on 'the show', but this time by Berio.

3 (i) A sf. ab from the Vle line of the Debussy links with the keyboards' punctuating chord.
(ii) S 2 uses Valéry, *Le cimetière marin*, line 4, to mark the perennial presence of the Debussy.

6 ab now effects the transition to:

7 Debussy, *La Mer*, III, *59* 10.

9 Str elaborate on Debussy's figuration.

11 Over the preceding extract, Tr 1 enters with the cor anglais figure from Debussy, *La Mer*, III, *18*.

12 The rest of the orchestra answer with *18* 2, save that Tr retain a dotted rhythm, running straight on into:

13 (i) Schoenberg, *loc. cit.*, again in the brass while:
(ii) the rest of the orchestra take up Mahler at Ma.463, which thus appears twenty-one bars late. This leads straight into:

BB

1 the climax of Mahler's movement, at which point his text is fully restored.

9 S 1 adds alternate, compressed chromatic phrases in solfège and scat.

CC

1 Mahler is again reduced to a series of fragments beneath sustained wind chords, with Timp providing the most immediate continuity.

13 (i) Again, the Mahler is lost save for a string fragment at **CC**15.

(ii) Eight-part wind, with Tr & Fl, Cor & Cl doubling at the octave, repeat three chords twice as Fl 1 moves from *d* to *g*.

(iii) Harp harmonics echo Ma.493 and, in **CC**17, Ma.497.

DD

1 Harp projects a pitch line from previous WW chords 1 & 2 (linked by their common *d*), followed two bars later by another linking the outer two pitches of 3, the inner two of 2, and the outer two of 1.

(ii) T 1 reverts to a series of fragments from Beck.7.

3 Vni C: Ma.501 (which is thus one bar late).

5 Tr, joined by other wind, initiates a final quote from *Der Rosenkavalier*, Act III, *295 7*.

9 Full orchestra joins in Strauss.

10 T 1: Beck.23.

12 T 1 announces Boulez quote at **EE**.

13 Punctuating chord acts as upbeat to:

EE

1 Boulez, 'Don' (= 'present') from *Pli selon pli,* opening chord.

6 Over the remains of the Boulez chord, WW quartet introduce the choral opening of Webern, *II. Kantate*, Op.31, 5th movement.

7 A quiet, aleatoric background is created, with Pf playing a passage from another work in the programme, while A 1, followed by S, revive the vocal imitation of instrumental parts first used at **H**.

9 Vn solo responds with its line from the Webern.

11 Sxf plays solo S part from the Webern.

14 Vn solo switches to Stockhausen, *Gruppen*, *22 3*, joined by other Str in the next bar.

17 A 1 & 2 sustain Harp *c* from Stockhausen, which is to become the dominant of Mahler's *f* minor at FF.

FF

1 (i) Instead of Stockhausen's chord, Berio uses his own punctuating chord for the last time.

(ii) Mahler returns (Ma.545), having lost 24 bars, and is tossed from voice to voice.

8 T 1 refers to title of Mahler (Resurrection Symphony).

13 T 1: the title of a German song, best known for the variations Sweelinck wrote upon it – though no reference to that work is intended here. Instead, it serves to underline that this is *not* a resurrection symphony: Berio's third movement, like all the others, ends with death.

GG

5 Vle shift by one semiquaver.

6 Hinted at by T 1's previous remark, the Mahler jumps ten bars from Ma.564 to Ma.575.

8 Vn A plays Ma.576 over Ma.577 from rest.

12 The final bar freezes into ceremonial, with gongs and an appropriate vote of thanks to the conductor.

5
Synthesis and Dissolution

The fourth movement

For a moment it seems as if Berio's commentary upon Mahler is to continue, for the fourth movement opens with the *db* and *eb* with which the vocalist enters at the start of the fourth movement of the Second Symphony. But there the similarity ends, for Berio, seeking a measure of symmetry around his central movement, engages upon a quiet, slow expansion from those two notes to four eight-part vocal chords that become increasingly invaded and enriched by instrumental additions. The latter provide the opportunity for reviving two features characteristic of the first movement: the exploration of a fixed harmonic 'object' by multiple voices moving at different rates, and the 'choral' differentiation of timbre groups.

The basic harmonic process is summarized in example 21. In each instance, the top five voices move upwards through a seven-note pitch sequence at differing rates, so that each is finally halted on a

Ex. 21

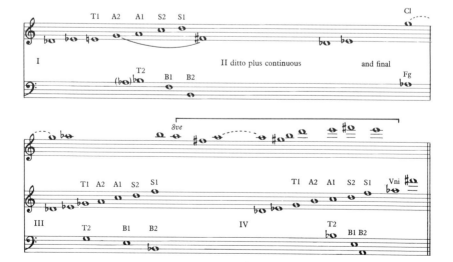

different note of the sequence, and the bottom three voices move downwards in similar fashion. Apart from their common starting-point, all the upward pitch sequences also have in common the c and d an octave above – preceded by an a in the first three cases, and followed by f in the last two.

Most of the other features of pitch organisation reflect Berio's concern with chromatic saturation. Thus in sections I and II the two notes that do not form part of the basic pitch process are given important subsidiary roles: the ab providing a temporary inflection of the harmony in the bass, and the sustained g in the alto voice finally resolving onto the missing $f\sharp$. Although in I the two initial notes are released as the voices progress towards their final chord, from II onwards a number of superimposed rhythms from instruments maintain a continuous oscillation between them.

This naturally underlines the move towards chromatic saturation as each chord reaches completion; accordingly at the end of II the bassoon re-enters with the transitory ab of a few bars before, and the violins C and clarinet re-establish a g an octave above the one that has just resolved onto an $f\sharp$. This high g initiates an independent melodic line, pursued well above the main textural aggregate but complementing its pitch processes. It thus provides the two notes missing from the chord built up in III: ab and b; and, having moved to an extreme register, includes the $g\sharp$ and $f\sharp$ missing from IV within its line – although now contrabassoon and bass tuba provide an ab at the other extremity, and violins in fact complete the twelve-note chord once the voices have come to rest.

Each chord has its characteristic spacing. I and II are coloured by alternating tones and minor thirds, with fourth and diminished fifth at the bottom. III consists of two diminished sevenths – one, more widely spaced, stretching down from db and the other, in close formation, moving up from eb – with the beginnings of the 'missing' diminished seventh chord added above the next tone grouping of c and d by the first and second sopranos, and completed by oboe and clarinet. IV, though less logically constructed, retains the characteristic spacing of larger intervals at the bottom (fifth and diminished fifth) with an aggregate based on thirds and seconds above them. But the harmonic growth of this final chord is in any case obscured by an upward moving chromatic cloud. There is thus a parsimonious growth in harmonic texture, complementing the gradual extension of harmonic gamut.

Rhythm and texture

The large-scale rhythmic framework is also extremely simple. The vocal parts of I and II are rhythmically identical, and both last thirty-seven minims. III abbreviates this to twenty-five, and IV compensates with forty-eight. But within this framework a gradual shift in emphasis and proportion is at work: in I and II there is a rough balance between the initial db/eb oscillation and the ensuing expansion, followed by a short final chord; III alters these pro-portions, for it is now the oscillation and the final stasis that are proportional, with a rapid expansion between them: IV (which is nearly twice the length of III) maintains similar proportions between oscillation and expansion, but throws all its weight onto the long-held final chord, passing it from choir to choir.

The instrumental oscillations of II and III, and the rising cluster of IV each use eight superposed rhythms that subdivide a common multiple (semibreve, breve and dotted breve respectively). As the common multiples become larger, so the selected subdivisions display more complex interrelations, producing a subtle growth in density of the rhythmic texture.

Unlike the calculated labyrinths of the first, third and fifth move-ments, the second and fourth movements, by virtue of their basic simplicity, invite the ear to dwell consistently upon the exercise of a specific form of sophistication: in the second movement that of a constantly shifting palette of harmonic colour, in the fourth move-ment a carefully controlled field of instrumental colour and texture. Berio's choice of instruments is fastidious – a re-assertion of his own sound-world after the parade of ancestral ghosts in the previous movement. Its central db/eb pedal provides a characteristic combina-tion: pitched percussion, tremolando string harmonics and flutter-tongue flutes, joined from **A2** by flutter-tongue trumpets, which have resumed their assorted mutes from the first movement. Their upward chromatic flurry at **B4** is amplified by flutter-tongue muted horns, a miniature recapitulation of the gesture that ended *Epifanie A*.

The text

Except in IV, the text consists of the phrase 'Rose de sang', phonetic materials derived from this phrase, and interpolated 'random sounds simulating very fast speech'. The words echo those of the fourth movement of Mahler's symphony – 'O Röschen roth' – but at the same time recall the gun-shot wounds that killed Martin Luther King and the theme of blood running through the first movement. IV reintroduces the 'appel bruyant/doux appel' opposition from the first movement, thereby ushering in the recapitulation of much of the verbal material from that movement in the finale; but it ends with another statement of the 'Rose' text.

The fifth movement

The fifth movement completes a shift in technical focus initiated by the second and third movements. The chamber version of *O King* accreted around itself elaborations of its own material to form the second movement; the third movement achieved a more elaborate (and destructive) commentary on Mahler's scherzo by seeking out relationships between that 'text' and other, heterogeneous materials. It is this search for similarities and common elements which now takes over as an autonomous principle. By means of it, Berio fuses together materials from all the previous movements into a new and vitriolic synthesis. The gesture seems deeply indebted to the nineteenth-century cult of organic completion. In practice, it offers neither apotheosis nor resolution, but rather an explosion of raw energy.

However, the search for structural analogies is also the underlying principle of Lévi-Strauss's *Le cru et le cuit*. Berio accordingly turns back to the verbal materials of the first movement, and proceeds to complete the processes initiated there. But again, what on a conceptual level implies a sense of ending on a practical, auditory level offers an open-ended stream of images only part-comprehensible at best.

In the first movement it was the internal structure of Lévi-Strauss's text that determined the musical structure of the vocal sections. Here, however, it is musical processes which have the upper hand

Ex. 22

	I	II	III	IV
	b/e			e/b
	E			
	b1			
	2=empty 7th			
A	1			
	2=filled 5th b			
B			b	b
	F		(=U)	
		e	A	b
	2			
C			B	
D	C 1			
	2			
		b i	C	
	1 and 2	ii		
		iii		
E			D	
			E	
			G	
			E	
		B i	I	
F		ii		
		iii	O	
			W	

75

Ex. 22

```
G
          C  i
             ii
H
             iii
                              I
          D  i
I
             ii
             iii
J    (2=empty 7th)
K
                        C
L
M
   L
N
O
   e
```

in determining large-scale form, with the text running in tandem. A detailed examination of the text can therefore be deferred for the moment. Although the musical processes are no longer articulated around a single, central text, the formal outlines of the movement are nevertheless determined by a series of dominant materials. At the heart of the movement lies *O King*. It is preceded by the alternating chords that opened the first movement, and is finally overtaken by a hectic orchestral monody reminiscent of, and finally merging into the one that closed the first movement. Around this basic structure are woven other recapitulated materials. Materials from the fourth movement alternate with those from the start of the first, while above them are presented fragments from the other two vocal sections from the first movement. Meanwhile a series of fragments encapsulating the progress of the third movement appear and dissolve back into the general *mêlée*. An outline of the way that these materials are disposed is set out in example 22. Rehearsal letters indicate the corresponding position in each movement; b = beginning, e = end. In the first-movement column, 1 and 2 denote the opening chords (see ex.3); in the second-movement column, i, ii and iii denote the three sections of its pitch set as described earlier (see ex.5). In the more detailed examination of these correspondences which follows, movements are referred to by Roman numerals, so that III **B**5 means: the fifth bar of **B** in the third movement. Material occurring before the first rehearsal letter of a movement is indicated just by bar number, so III 5 denotes the fifth bar of that movement.

Before 'O King'

The movement opens with three superposed and partly related layers. The piano's rhapsodic idiom derives from its solo at the end of the first movement, but it now incorporates a series of fleeting allusions. It starts from the final chord of IV, but immediately follows it with elements of chord 1 from I (anticipating the return of that chord as an explicit reference-point in V 13). From b.6 onwards the two chords are made to interact. But I 1 also has an eb in common with the db/eb oscillation of IV; the hint of this in V 1 will be fully realized in V 12–13. The eb also summons up recollections of the eb/d alternation characteristic of I's instrumental section (cf. I **J8–L1**). Echoes of that appear in V 6 and V 8. Above this, the flute expands upon its solo from the last four bars of I, embellishing it with the oscillating thirds from the Fire section of that movement (I **E4**), to which more explicit reference will be made at V 10. The voice meanwhile provides a new setting of the text from IV **B1–C6**, though inverting its order so as to end with Lévi-Strauss in preparation for the main body of the movement. The close relation of the vocal line to the flute part is made explicit in V 6–8; and it ends (V 8–9) with a fleeting allusion to the monody which is to end the movement (cf. **J5**).

After this prelude, the voices enter at V 10 to initiate a more substantive set of relations, summarized in example 23. They employ the familiar db/eb oscillation from IV 1 which dissolves into chord 1 from I in the strings at V 13, linked by their common eb. Above them, the flute oscillations are now answered by clarinet and saxophone – the original protagonists of I's Fire section. They do not, however, play at their original pitches (cf. I **E4**). Instead all three now complement the pitch content of chord 1, achieving chromatic saturation except for the b. This appears in the answering tremolo from piano and harpsichord – a skeletal version of chord 2 (cf. I 3). A further substitute for this chord is provided a few bars later when chord 1, reinstated at **A1** and shot through with attacks from wind choirs, implodes upon itself to form a saturated fifth, $c–g$, at **A6**. Berio has thus sketched out the first two of three alternations between chords 1 and 2 that make up the first Water section in I. These chords now move into abeyance for a few bars before returning to complete the reworking of that section.

Ex. 23

Having established its relation to chord 1, the $d\flat/e\flat$ oscillation now returns to demonstrate similar relations to two other chords (thus mirroring its expansion into three different chords in IV). The first of these also serves to underline its origins in the opening bars of 'Urlicht', the fourth movement of Mahler's Second Symphony. During IV, the two notes had always avoided the resolution onto f that completes the phrase in the Mahler.[1] Now, however, brass sforzandi are employed to spell out the progress from $d\flat$ to f.[2] But $d\flat\ e\flat\ f$ is also the retrograde of the first three notes of the chord that ends II which the voices recapitulate, at **B7**, before resolving onto a more mellifluous six-part chord incorporating the d–a basis of chord 1. At **B9** they return for the last time to the $d\flat/e\flat$ oscillation, resolving into a complete version of chord 2 from I. This in turn ushers in the final move from the expanded version of chord 1 (cf. I **C1**) to chord 2 at **D1–3**.

Superposed on this basic layer are other elements called back into play by a process of association. The pitches $d\flat$ and $e\flat$ figure largely in the staccato bass notes accompanying the second Water section at I **F4**. Accordingly, the chord 4 cluster reappears, at **B2–13**, both in its original form and as reinterpreted in III **U1–5**, thereby completing the imploded recapitulation of materials from I. Similarly, the filled fifth c–g at **A6** is quietly answered by another, b–$f\sharp$, from the electronic organ at **B2**. Not only does this complement the filled third, $g\flat$–$b\flat$ of the second Water section from I, here etched out by trumpets and piccolo clarinet, but it also reinstates the harmonic background to the start of III, from which fragments begin to be heard. Thus at **B** the harp plays its initial quotation from *La Mer*, followed by a snatch of Hindemith (**B2**), of Mahler's introduction (**B4**, cor anglais), the upbeat to the main theme of the movement (**B5**, strings), and the explosion that originally followed nine bars later (**B6**, full orchestra plus clarinets). From then on until **D**, Hindemith fragments constantly invade the texture, thereby preparing for the important role that they are going to play later on in the movement.

From **B** to **D** the texture is also shot through with explosive attacks from piccolo, brass and percussion that are to remain a unifying feature of the movement through to the final section. At this point (though not necessarily hereafter) the brass attacks serve to underline pitch processes already discussed, while the piccolo line keeps its own, non-systematic independence.

Materials from 'O King'

At **D** a reworking of the outburst from I **C** ushers in a restatement of the principal line from II, which conserves the interaction of pitch and rhythmic sets (the latter, due to the slower tempo, now counted in semiquavers rather than quavers) through to the point where the

---

[1] Instead, it resolved onto e, $g\flat$ and g respectively.
[2] cf. Altmann 1977, p.54.

principal voice abandons the articulation of that interaction (I9, cf. II D12). The four relevant statements of the pitch cycle are thus placed as follows: **A** begins at **D3**, **B** at **E8**, **C** at **G3** and **D** at **H10**. The more complex context in which this line is now placed entails a few minor alterations, but apart from a moment of textural confusion in which the *a* of section Aiii is blurred (D11–12), the pitch set remains intact throughout. Two minor glosses upon it are introduced: the long-held final *b♭* of section Aiii is temporarily deflected to a *b♮* (E7), and in statement **B** a *g♯* is introduced to mediate between the *b*s and *c♯*s of sections Bi and Bii (F1 and F5). Similarly, the rhythmic set maintains a semiquaver version of example 10a in all but a few instances. The blurring of *a* in section Aiii provokes a parallel dislocation in the rhythmic set with the aggregate 7 of *f+a* being extended to 9. There are also long pauses on the *g♯* of section Aiii (E2) and the *f* of section Ci (G3) as other materials are dealt with; and the *a* of section Ciii is abbreviated from 4 to 2 to provide a more powerful sequence (H4).

Of the rest of the structure of *O King* only vestigial fragments remain, and these are in any case transformed by their context. Thus the interplay of attacks within each note takes on a quite new character through the reappearance of flutter-tongue flutes and trumpets, plus rolled [r]s and rapid alternation between consonants in the voices, periodically abetted by bongos. The hectic tone imparted by this use of rapid repetition increases with each cycle of the pitch series. By section Biii (F2) rapidly tongued winds have joined in. At the start of statement **C** (G2) the three percussionists abandon bongos for snare drums and underline the brass as they crescendo into, or fiercely attack each note of the pitch cycle. The sforzandos which in *O King* mapped out a macrocosmic version of the pitch cycle are now applied to every note – initially by piano and/or saxophone, eventually by multiple brass. Although, as before, anticipations and prolongations blur one note into the next, there is no extended or sophisticated use of selective resonance: any such exercise would merely render the already dense texture opaque. The unselective sustaining of notes that occurs in statement **C** is a reflection of other harmonic processes and is best discussed with them. There are likewise clear traces of some of the extraneous pitches; but these, too, are best discussed in relation to their new context.

Superposed materials

The harmonic materials that accrete around the pitch cycle are summarized in example 24, excluding the numerous fragments recapitulated from the third movement, the sporadic outbursts of fff attacks from piccolo, percussion and brass, and during statement **D** the introductory fragments from the ensuing monody – all of which will be discussed below. Black note-heads indicate elements that sound only briefly against the specified note of the pitch cycle. As in the second movement, there is a steady increase in harmonic density; but here the progression is dramatized by sharper distinctions between each statement. Thus while statement **A** uses chord 1 and 2 from the first movement, statement **B** introduces other mainly eight-note chords whose spacing and intervallic content are similar to those of chord 1 and to the three terminal chords from the fourth movement. Although statement **C** increases the harmonic density of the accompanying chords, its most striking feature is the introduction of sequentially built chromatic clusters, in preparation for statement **D** where cluster attacks alternate registers in a manner reminiscent of the start of the third movement. Meanwhile, the pitch cycle complements the processes at work in the commentary, building aggregates in **Cii** and being presented throughout statement **D** by the piano in parallel clusters.

Much of this material is related to the pitch cycle by the familiar principles of common pitches and chromatic complementarity. The

Ex. 24

process is clearly seen in cycle **A**, where the *b* common to the pitch series and chord 2 is constantly underlined. Apart from that *b*, chord 2 contains three of the five pitches excluded from the pitch cycle, which it almost disrupts when, at **D10**, it is used to link the *b*s of **Aii** and **Aiii**. Beneath the latter, the chord is extended by a series of thirds down to *d*, producing a cross with chord 1, and then drawn up again. Chord 1 shares both *c♯* and *b♭*with the pitch cycle; it is associated with the former in its first two appearances and with the latter in its last appearance.

The two pitches excluded from the pitch cycle that are not part of chord 2, *f♯* and *e*, reappear along with *c* at their original octave placement from 'O King' during statements **B** and **C**. In each case their presence is emphasised by low brass and woodwind (at **F3**, **G4** and **H**). Apart from those and two brief recurrences of chord 2, new harmonic materials invade the last three statements of the cycle. At first, they contain several common elements: a *b♭* bass and a middle *c* and *e* recur throughout statement **B**; and an ostinato *c♯/d* alternation runs from **Bii** to the end of **Biii**. The *g/f♯* alternation set up there serves as a further unifying factor until **Ciii**; but by this time harmonic constants have given way to cluster attacks – some having one extremity in common with the pitch cycle, others not.

The quotation fragments from the third movement continue throughout this section. An outline of their progress can be seen from example 22; but a more detailed concordance is provided in example 25. One or two deviations apart, they summarize the progress of the third movement from the first appearance of the Hindemith *Kammermusik* at the start of the movement to its reappearance at **W**. The only point at which the sequence is broken is just after the start of the **B** cycle (**E8**), where a transposed Debussy fragment comments upon the introduction to Mahler's *col legno* reprise of the main theme, and the more extensive solo violin quotation reveals an affinity by inversion with the familiar fragment from *Agon*. As in the third movement, the fragments sometimes share notes in common with their 'text', and sometimes pursue their own tangential path. Meanwhile the fff attacks from brass, piccolo and percussion consolidate their previous function as markers of significant structural events. They announce each section of each of first three statements of the pitch cycle, except for **Bii** and **Ciii** – the latter being marked by an attack chord from the brass. By statement **D** explosions abound, making such markers undistinctive.

The final monody

At **H7**, as statement **C** comes to an end, the Hindemith fragment played by clarinet and piccolo is answered by oboe and cor anglais with the opening descent from an undulating pitch sequence that is to generate the final monody. The fragment recurs at **I**, extended to form a complete undulation; and throughout the rest of statement **D** further fragments appear between the punctuating chords (at **I5** and

Ex. 25

Movement V	=	Movement III
B Harp		5
B2 Vc		**A**11 Vni B and **U** (=Movement I, **F**3)
B6		**A**12
B7 Ob & Fl		**A**20 Vn solo
B8ff		**A**20
B9–13		**U**–**U**4
C Ott & Cl picc		**B**7
D3 Vn solo		**C**10
D4 Ob		**B**5 (approx.)
D7		**C**15
D8 Ob		**C**16
D9 Cl picc		**C**8
D11 Fag		**C**23
D12 Vni		**D**9 (reworked)
D12 Fl		**D**22
E Vni		**D**19
E2 Cl picc		**E**19
E4		**G**9 (reworked)
E6		**G**15
E8 Ob & C.i.		**E**6
E9 Str		**I**6 and **E**2
F6		**O**5 and **O**7
F7		**W**2
G2		**W**5
G3		**W**7
H3		**W**15
H10		**I**6
K6 Vni B		**C**3

from I7 on – their derivation will be discussed below). Finally at J the monody begins. Although modelled stylistically on its counterpart in the first movement, it is based on a quite distinct pitch process. Where the first movement recalled the virtual counterpoints, oscillations and tremolandi of *Sequenza VI*, this one establishes a 'wave-form' pitch set, covering the gamut of the treble and bass staves – an idea that was to be further developed in *Bewegung* (1971) and *Eindrücke* (1974).

It consists of three down-up undulations – here labelled a, b and c – which appear in three progressively longer forms set out as 1, 2 and 3 in example 26. In their various occurrences, each undergoes minor modifications which are set out on separate staves below or above the 'principal' version. 1 is first stated complete from J1–5. 2a follows in bars J6 and J9, interspersed with other materials to be discussed below; but the $f\,c\sharp$ of what should be the start of 2b at J12 instead short-circuits back to 1, followed by a full statement of 2 from J14–16. It is directly followed by a first statement of 3 (J16–L1); and like the first statement of 2a at J6–9, it is a fragmented one. But from the first entry of 3c at L the impetus is continuous: first a final restatement of 2 (L1–4), modified to bring its pitch content into closer line with 3; and then two restatements of 3 (L5–9 and L9–M4) that lead into a reworking of the final bars of the first movement, discussed below.

No simple additive process leads from version 1 to version 3. Comparing section b, and the lower extremity of a in each version, it can be seen that although both 1 and 2 are contained in 3, 1 is not contained in 2. In any case, it is 3 which displays the most striking internal organisation. 3a combines a retrograded pitch sequence with an inverted interval sequence – each accommodating the other by interpolated notes. (Only two notes belong within neither process: the bottom a which creates a retrograde inversion of the three-note peak at the end of 3a and 3b; and the g of the descent, whose insertion creates a $c\sharp\,g\,e\,e\flat$ complement to the subsequent $e\,b\,a\,f\sharp\,f$.) 3b contents itself with a simpler rationale, transposing two pitch-class sequences by an octave to create a satisfyingly varied retrograde. With 3c, internal cogency gives way to allusion: the descent is the first movement's chord 1, with an added $g\sharp$ to spell out the solitary major third, and a preceding g to complete the higher 'diminished seventh'. The ascent combines elements of chord 2 with an allusion to the corresponding moment in 3a.

Version 2's simpler profile allows for further harmonic allusions, albeit in a form that is not so explicit. The descent of 2b from g to the low $a\flat$ again contains elements of the first movement's chord 1, now transposed down an augmented fourth, while the ascent from that $a\flat$ to $d\flat$ [ ] $a\,b$ is derived from the opening chord of the fourth movement, transposed down a minor third, and with first and second alto parts replaced by a solitary f. The structural simplicity of 3b relative to 3a is explained if it is viewed as an elaboration of the

Ex. 26

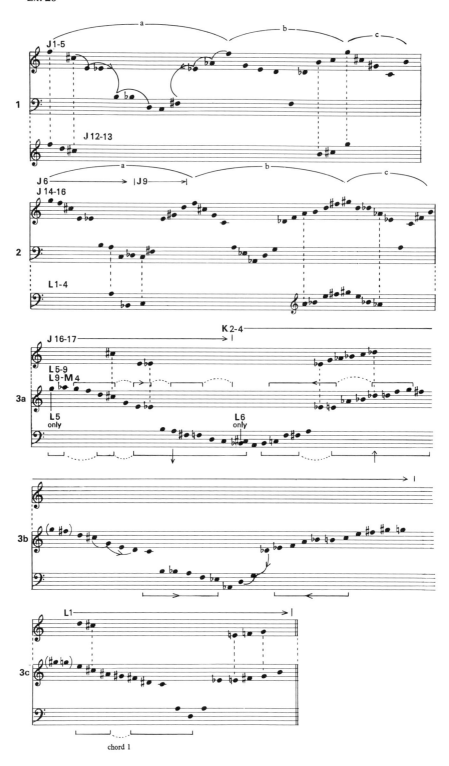

harmonically allusive 2b. But 2a and 2c seem to be straightforward reductions of the corresponding parts of 3. Version 1 is an even more drastic reduction of 3 – so much so, that it can afford to create its own internal logic, most notably in the intervallic retrograde of 1a, part of which then serves to link the ascent of 1a to the descent of 1b. The $f\,db\,[\ ]\,c$ of 1b's ascent stands in an analogous relationship to the $g\,[\ ]\,f\sharp c$ of 1c's descent; and a further two-interval module unifies the descent of 1a when $f\,c\sharp\,e$ is followed by $eb\,b\,[\ ]\,d$.

The fragments that announce the onset of the monody are all straightforwardly derived. As was noted above, those at H7 and I derive from 1a, as does a further fragment at I5 (clarinet). It is followed at I7 (oboe) by the start of 2a, and at I8 by a composite figure derived from the peak between 1b and 1c, modified to prepare for the $f/c\sharp$ oscillation that starts the first full statement of 1.

As with its predecessor in the first movement, the momentum of the monody is at first checked by a series of pauses – here filled with vocal duets which recall the idiom of the soprano's opening solo (and indeed begin and end with references to it) but employ pitch materials from the monody. In the first hiatus at J5, the final $c\,b$ from 1 is simply answered by part of the initial descent from 3a, passing from saxophone to first alto – a gesture already familiar from b.8–9 of the movement. But at J7 the duetting begins: first T 1 and B 1, both basing themselves on 2b; then A 1 mixing 1a with 2a transposed up an octave, and T 2 initially retrograding 3a. The monody gathers momentum, but is again interrupted at J17, where T 1 combines 1a and 2a, while B 1 anticipates the continuation of 3a. Finally, at K4, oboe and cor anglais play the two parts of 3a simultaneously, thus emphasising the pitch retrogrades of example 26, and the sopranos echo their final notes as background to a last Mahlerian reminiscence. S 1 extends this into a variant upon her opening phrase from this movement, whereupon the monody takes over with uninterrupted impetus.

At first, the monody's harmonic clarity is clouded only by a background of glissando chords from the strings (whose internal structures recall – but do not reproduce – that of chord 4 from the first movement, cf. ex.3). Brass sforzandi, carried over from the final statement of the 'O King' pitch set, underline individual notes – though not to pick out any pitch sequence of autonomous significance. However, from L onwards a process of thickening analogous to that of the first movement monody begins: first octaves, then fifths (L7, oboe), then thirds (L8, flute 1). At the same time, extensive cluster-based chords similar to those underlying the latter two statements of the 'O King' pitch set emerge: first in the background at L3 (strings), and then dominating the texture from L6 to M, where the configuration in brass and strings 'takes off' in parallel motion to the monody. The monody itself begins to generate its own harmonic backdrop from L9 on, where individual fifth-spaced instrumental couples sustain their notes until the monody again rises to catch them up into the general *mêlée*.

At the final semiquaver of **M4**, the monody flows into a reworking of the final, climactic bars from the first movement (cf. I **L**). Within the climax itself, the pattern of pauses between outbursts is rearranged, and two of the individual gestures are repeated. As a result of the reworked pattern only a portion of the piano part is retained. But the voices' final statement of chords 1 and 2 is substantially lengthened, with the oscillating flute answered as at the start of the movement, though this time by oboe and piano. Along with the pizzicato bass line of the last five bars, they provide the complementary pitches to the long-held final chord, 2, which is passed from one instrumental choir to another in a series of quiet attacks. But to the end impetus is maintained by three snare drums and high strings. As in the first movement, three gongs signal the end.

Text and music

The relationship between text and music in this movement is, in outline, simple. Fire and water materials alternate from b.5 up to the final notes of statement **A** of the pitch cycle (E8). From after the fermata at E2 up to the end of the 'O King' cycles at **J**, the voices concentrate on materials from the four interrelated myths shown in example 1: at first the M.2/M.125 relationship, which dominates the second statement of the cycle; and thereafter, from **G**, the relations between M.124 and the 'missing' M.1, which occupy the third and fourth cycle. As the final monody enters at **J** so, too, do new myth materials that focus irrevocably on the underlying theme of the whole work: 'la vie brève'.

Other materials are added to complicate this straightforward pattern. There are occasional interjections derived from the Beckett text of the third movement. But the most notable and idiosyncratic of these additions is a series of four analytical observations taken from Lévi-Strauss's text and rewritten by Berio so as to apply to music. They are set out below:

Berio	Lévi-Strauss
	α
Partiel ou provisoire,	Partiel et provisoire,
ce dernier commentaire	l'ébauche de synthèse où nous
	a mené la deuxième partie
n'est pas convainçant,	n'est pas absolument convainçante,
car il laisse de côté	car elle laisse de côté
d'importants aspects	d'importants fragments
de nos thèmes. (**B**13–14)	du mythe de référence, (p.155)

β

Mais pourtant les thèmes sont là,	Pourtant les mythes sont là,
qui affirment la priorité	qui affirment la priorité
de la discontinuité universelle	de la discontinuité universelle
des thèmes sur la continuité	des espèces sur la continuité
de l'organisation interne	interne du chromatisme
à chacuns. (D7–9, F2–G3)	particulier à chacune. (p.330)

γ

Avant de terminer	Avant d'en terminer
d'une façon provisoirement	provisoirement
définitive (à Vienne on dit	avec les codes sensoriels,
'définitivement provisoire')	
il faudrait resoudre	il est indispensable de resoudre
quelque contradiction (E2)	une contradiction. (p.168)

δ

Partout, ailleurs, les thèmes	Partout ailleurs, les codes sensoriels
inversent la valeur	inversent régulièrement la valeur
de leur termes	de leurs termes,
selon qu'il s'agit	selon qu'il s'agit
de retarder la mort	de retarder la mort
ou d'assurer la résurrection (E2)	ou d'assurer la résurrection.(p.171)

This curious procedure might lead one to suppose that, like certain of the Beckett quotations in the third movement, these are to be used to comment on specific musical events. Some of them can be interpreted in that way – notably α , which is generically appropriate within this context. Passage β was originally a discussion of how different bird feathers are recognized as belonging to specific species rather than being allotted a place in the colour spectrum; and in its new version it might be taken as a comment on the various quotations from the third movement, which listeners will identify according to their source rather than in terms of common technical features. But γ and δ , which appear simultaneously at E2, are frankly indecipherable in musical terms. One is inclined to conclude that if Berio was intent upon working at the limits of comprehensibility, then these fragments of analytical mumbo-jumbo were placed deliberately beyond it.

Fire vs. Water

The insertion of these materials clouds an otherwise simple process. Materials representing the fire myth M.9 – in all cases but one the familiar 'appel bruyant/ doux appel' – alternate with the other myths to which it is related by homologous triads (see above, p.11). One of these, Lévi-Strauss's 'mythe de référence' M.1, was notably absent from the first movement; and it is this which first alternates with M.9, though always presented in tandem with its familiar transformational opposite, M.124. They emerge from the phonetic undergrowth at b.13, as chord 1 from the first movement establishes itself; but they manage only a few words before they are cut off. They are even further pruned when they reappear at **B**9, and thereafter temporarily retire. Meanwhile the voices pursue an encapsulated recapitulation of those materials in the first movement (I **D–H**5) related by other homologous triads, though the 'eau céleste/ terrestre' opposition that divided them is now absent. This runs from **B**12 to **E**, and completes M.9's alternation with the various water myths.

Berio now isolates a single opposition ('un fils privé de mère/ nourriture') from Lévi-Strauss's table analysing relations between M.2 and M.125,[3] a selection from whose contents had been recited at a gallop in the first movement; and he develops it as an extended lyric setting. This starts at **E**4 and occupies the whole of the second statement of the pitch set from the second movement.

M.1 vs. M.124

From **G** to **H** the voices start a simultaneous narration of the analogous openings of M.1 and M.124: in M.1 a single young man, in M.124 the elder brothers of Asaré, each rape their mother and are punished by their father. Berio then proceeds to a simultaneous comparison of other features from the two myths. In each, the hero is protected from a potentially mortal encounter (in M.1 with the arrows of maleficent 'souls', in M.124 with crocodiles) by three helpful birds or animals. Each episode is summarized in numbered succession. Berio then enumerates other points of comparison: fourth (**I**1–2), that both heros hunt lizards (with disastrous results: from one batch of lizards is born the pursuing crocodile (M.124), while the other decomposes, attracting vultures who eat the hero's buttocks); fifth (**I**5–7), the unexpected results of immersion (Asaré's brothers, after bathing, are changed into stars, whereas the vengeful father of M.1's hero, finally thrown into the lake by his son, is eaten by fish, his lungs turning into aquatic plants); and sixth (**I**10), helpful relations (though since Asaré's uncle is a skunk, the association between what appears to be urination and what appears to be phallic symbolism is yet another example of semantic proliferation from isolated fragments).

'La vie brève'

As the pitch set comes to a halt, at **I**10, so too does the comparison between M.1 and M.124. In the final monody the voices move on to new materials but a long-familiar theme. At **J** the second soprano begins a fresh narration, that of M.87. This tells of how cultivated plants, like the fire of M.9, must be paid for by 'la vie brève'. She stops almost immediately to give way to another myth whose origins have yet to be traced (it does not appear in *Le cru et le cuit* nor in any other part of *Mythologiques*) but whose theme is clearly also that of human mortality. Like the myth narration at the

---

[3] Lévi-Strauss 1964, p.215.

start of the first movement, it is interrupted at the crucial moment, just as we are about to learn what consolation the 'esprit special' is to bring to mortal man. The voices throw themselves into a frenetic exchange of mainly plosive consonants before resolving into a final statement of the image underlying the whole work: 'péripétie': 'héros tué'.

6
Epilogue

Any score provokes two divergent aesthetic responses. The first, more readily acknowledged by tradition, is that of perceiving sounds structured in (and lost in) time. The second is the aesthetic pleasure of exploring the score itself: a counterpoint between visual pattern, knowledge of the rules of the game, and the sometimes hallucinatory suggestions of the inner ear, played out within a time-warp where the synchronic can become diachronic, and vice versa.

As far as contemporary composers are concerned, the divide between these two aesthetics becomes most obvious in the examination of musical process and structure, for in many contemporary works there is a wide discrepancy between aural impressions of informality and the meticulous logics of the score. But although there is more in the harmonic and rhythmic organisation of *Sinfonia* than meets the ear, the gap here is not a wide one. Berio's choice of musical language is deliberately simple and graphic, and it operates within a circumscribed range of technical concerns. Yet the verbal materials, with the exception of 'O King', not only mark out a wider discrepancy between the listener's ear and the score-reader's eye, but deliberately underline a further gap between those things that become obvious from looking at the score and those that can be made clear only by referring beyond it. This coupling of vivid, directly comprehensible musical gestures and partly baffling verbal fragments is entirely characteristic of Berio. It reverses the situation all too frequently found in contemporary music of a linear, coherent text that holds together a rather loose agglomeration of musical ideas. For Berio uses explicit musical processes to establish continuity and security, while allowing words, half grasped, to provoke a state of aesthetic risk where intuitive sense may or may not emerge amongst the isolated images of a semantic non-sequitur.

In thus transforming the playing upon words so dear to Joyce in *Finnegans Wake* – making layer upon layer of superposed material sound together around a musical or verbal core – Berio reactivates one of the central experiences of the 'modernist' tradition. The listener, troubled by the rich confusion of what he has heard, may well seek refuge in the score; but there he will discover a maze of allusions to things beyond the score. The more avidly he seeks to pin these down, the more clear will it become that there is no logical end to his activities. But this moment of scholastic exasperation (richly familiar to students of Joyce, or Pound, or Borges) serves to underline the necessity of coming to grips with that initial confusion in another, and complementary way – that of learning to be receptive to the peculiarly vivid aesthetic impact of the half-understood. Seen thus, the ellipses and allusions of the 'modernist' tradition, and the verbal and musical superpositions of Berio's own work offer not gratuitous mystification, but a survival kit against the facile nihilism that so easily informs attempts to analyse a disjointed, relativistic environment in which 'the unexpected is always upon us'. The more determinedly a study such as this seeks to track down allusions, to trace formal processes, the more clamorously does it evoke the necessity for its complementary mode of perception. The exposition of art as artefact is a necessary moment of demystification – for by suggesting how it was put together, it challenges you to consider what it would be like to do something similar – but it is only useful if it can serve as a springboard back to the limits of the comprehensible, where many things sound at once.

Bibliography

Altmann, Peter. *Sinfonia von Luciano Berio: eine analytische Studie*. Universal Edition, Vienna, 1977.

Bauer-Lechner, Natalie. *Recollections of Gustav Mahler*. Translation by Dika Newlin of *Erinnerungen an Gustav Mahler* (Leipzig, 1923) with notes by Peter Franklin. Faber Music with Faber & Faber, London, 1980.

Beckett, Samuel. *The Unnamable*. Translation, by the author, of *L'innommable* (Paris, 1952). John Calder, London, 1958; new edition by Calder & Boyars, London, 1975.

Berio, Luciano. 'Poesia e musica – un 'esperienza'. *Incontri musicali: Quaderni internazionali di musica contemporanea*, iii (1959), 98ff. French translation in *Contrechamps*, i: *Luciano Berio* (1983), 24–35.

——. 'Meditation on a Twelve-tone Horse'. *Christian Science Monitor*, 15 July 1968. French translation in *Contrechamps*, i: *Luciano Berio* (1983), 46–50.

——. *Two Interviews*. Translation by David Osmond-Smith of *Intervista sulla musica* (Bari, 1981). Marion Boyars, London, 1985.

Budde, Elmar. 'Zum dritten Satz der Sinfonia von Luciano Berio'. *Die Musik der sechziger Jahre: zwölf Versuche*, ed. Rudolf Stephan, 128–44. Schott, Mainz, 1972.

Dressen, Norbert. *Sprache und Musik bei Luciano Berio: Untersuchungen zu seiner Vokalcompositionen*. Gustav Bosse, Regensburg, 1982.

Flynn, George W. 'Listening to Berio's Music'. *The Musical Quarterly*, lxi (1975), 388–421.

Hicks, Michael. 'Text, Music, and Meaning in Berio's *Sinfonia*, 3rd Movement'. *Perspectives of New Music*, xx (1981–2), 199–224.

International Phonetic Association. *The Principles of the International Phonetic Association*. I.P.A., London, 1949.

Jahnke, Sabine. 'Materialien zu einer Unterrichtssequenz: Des Antonius von Padua Fischpredigt bei Orff–Mahler–Berio'. *Musik und Bildung*, v (1973), 615–22.

Krieger, Georg, and Wolfgang Martin Stroh. 'Probleme der Collage in der Musik, aufgezeigt am 3. Satz der Sinfonia von Luciano Berio'. *Musik und Bildung*, iii (1971), 229–35.

Lévi-Strauss, Claude. *Le cru et le cuit*. Plon, Paris, 1964. English translation by John and Doreen Weightman as *The Raw and the Cooked*. Jonathan Cape, London, 1970.

Lyons, John (ed.). *New Horizons in Linguistics*. Penguin, Harmondsworth, 1970.

Mitchell, Donald. *Gustav Mahler: the Wunderhorn Years.* Faber & Faber, London, 1975.

Nattiez, Jean-Jacques. 'Rencontre avec Lévi-Strauss'. *Musique en jeu,* xii (1973), 3–9.

Osmond-Smith, David. 'From Myth to Music: Lévi-Strauss's *Mythologiques* and Berio's *Sinfonia'. The Musical Quarterly,* lxvii (1981), 230–60.

——. 'Joyce, Berio et l'art de l'explosition'. *Contrechamps,* i: *Luciano Berio* (1983), 83–9.

Ravizza, Victor. 'Sinfonia für acht Singstimmen und Orchester von Luciano Berio'. *Melos,* xli (1974), 291–7.

Ruwet, Nicolas. *Langage, musique, poésie.* Editions du Seuil, Paris, 1972.

Sanguineti, Edoardo. 'Laborintus II'. *Contrechamps,* i: *Luciano Berio* (1983), 75–82.

Stoianova, Iwanka. 'Verbe et son, centre et absence'. *Musique en jeu,* xvi (1974), 79–102.

Tibbe, Monika. *Über die Verwendung von Liedern und Liedelementen in instrumentalen Symphoniesätzen Gustav Mahlers.* Emil Katzbichler, Munich, 1971.

Index

94